Women at Work

Deborah Clarke is a Management Consultant, Associate Fellow of the British Psychological Society, and a Chartered Psychologist with a special interest in occupational and counselling psychology. She has been involved in promoting good practice in organizations for nearly fifteen years via training, consultancy and a range of publications. She now works predominantly with senior staff members and teams around cultural change, managing cultural diversity, team building and management development. She enjoys working in the area of personal and organizational transformation, with individual managers, and staff teams, as well as working collaboratively on large-scale change programmes. She has published extensively, and this, her latest book, explores the issues facing women at work in the 1990s.

Women at Work

AN ESSENTIAL GUIDE
FOR THE WORKING WOMAN

DEBORAH CLARKE

ELEMENT

Shaftesbury, Dorset ● Rockport, Massachusetts
Brisbane, Queensland

Published in Great Britain in 1992 by
Element Books Limited
Longmead, Shaftesbury, Dorset

Published in the USA in 1992 by
Element, Inc
42 Broadway, Rockport, MA 01966

Published in Australia in 1992 by
Element Books Ltd for
Jacaranda Wiley Ltd
33 Park Road, Milton, Brisbane, 4064

Cover photographs courtesy the Ace Photo Agency
Front top left © Gabe Palmer
Front top centre © John David Begg
Front top right © Gabe Palmer
Front bottom left © Mark French
Front bottom centre © Mauritius
Front bottom right © Gabe Palmer

Cover design by Max Fairbrother
Designed by Roger Lightfoot
Typeset by Poole Typesetting (Wessex) Ltd, Dorset
Printed and bound in Great Britain by
Dotesios, Trowbridge

British Library Cataloguing in Publication
data available

Library of Congress Cataloguing in Publication
data available

ISBN 1–85230–109–0

66 120164 7 104566

Contents

To all the women I have worked with
who have taught me what I know.

Acknowledgements

I would like to express my thanks to Julia McCutchen, Commissioning Editor, for her support and encouragement throughout, and to Felicity Carter, Freelance Editor, for her useful comments and suggestions on the first draft. At the same time, for all the love and support I received from the Post-graduate group at the School of Management, Bath University, who knew I could do it, thank you!

Thanks also to all those who have allowed me to quote extracts from their work and specifically to the following individuals and publishers for permission to quote from their works.

Assertion Training, Stress Management and *Management Effectiveness for Women*. Reproduced by permission of National Extension College, 18 Brooklands Avenue, Cambridge CB2 2HN. Tel: (0223) 316644.

Body and Soul by Anita Roddick. Copyright © 1991 The Body Shop plc and Russell Miller. Reprinted by permission of Random Century and Crown Publishers, Inc.

How to Get Control of Your Time and Your Life by Alan Lakein. Copyright © 1973 by Alan Lakein. Reprinted by permission of Gower Publishing Group and David McKay Company, a division of Random House, Inc.

Managing Stress by David Fontana, British Psychology Society and Routledge, 1990.

Prospering Woman by Ruth Ross. Copyright © 1982 Ruth Ross. Reprinted with permission of New World Library, San Rafael, California.

1001 Ways to Save the Planet by Bernadette Vallely, Penguin Books, 1990. Copyright © Bernadette Vallely, 1990.

Introduction

MORE WOMEN IN PAID EMPLOYMENT

During the 1990s significantly more women will be entering or re-entering the labour market, and working at all levels within any organization. This influx will force workplaces − be they large multi-nationals, public sector organizations or small local businesses − to become more 'women-friendly' in their practices. Job sharing, flexitime, workplace crêches, and help with managing the career break, are likely to become standard. In the meantime, even though women make up to approximately 40 per cent of the labour force, many workplaces can still appear rather inhospitable, with little account being taken of their needs as workers.

> To enter, prosper and survive within an organization can depend upon how a person is viewed by decision makers; whether the person is viewed as a full organizational member, as someone who 'fits in', as a 'committed' person. This scenario is highly problematic for women given that they are too often viewed as having a primary commitment to a domestic life outside the organization.[1]

Given that organizations can be quite difficult places for women, why is it that so many more will be entering paid employment, either for the first time, or after childrearing? The reasons include economic necessity, changes in the nature of work, and women's expectations and lifestyle. Increasingly women expect to be employed for significant periods of their lives, either because they want to be economically independent, or because their wage-earning capacity is essential to their well-being, or to that of their family. This is particularly true for the growing number who head up single-parent families, and women in partnerships where the male earner is unable to generate sufficient income to meet basic needs. 'It is not simply that aspirations have risen, but rather that it is the incomes of wives which keep many families above the poverty line.'[2] This is reinforced by a survey of EEC countries, which suggested that a substantial proportion of married women employees were at work because of 'necessity' or 'insufficient salary of the spouse'.[3]

Many women no longer expect or want to be defined solely in terms of the traditional roles of wife and mother, and are increasingly looking to paid employment for their self-fulfilment. At the same time, organizational and technological changes have created a dearth of semi-skilled white-collar and manual occupations, and women have slipped into such positions.

So for most women, working outside the home has become, or will become, a permanent way of life. Given that this is the case women, particularly school or college leavers and returners, need to think seriously about what they want from the world of work, and be aware of the consequences of decisions taken concerning subject choices at school, examination or courses followed, and jobs accepted. If paid employment is the reality for most women, they need to take a stronger stand in the world of work, and decide whether they want to be a 'core' worker of the future, a 'portfolio' person or a member of the 'flexible labour force', as outlined by Charles Handy in *The Age of Unreason*, which we shall talk about in more detail later.

This book aims to present some ideas and identify some skills to help women, particularly women returners, manage their own transformation into the world of work, whilst acknowledging that the nature of work itself is going through a major change.

CHANGES IN THE WORLD OF WORK

What are these changes, and how are they likely to affect women at work? According to Charles Handy, the trend for businesses to become leaner and more streamlined, started in the 1980s, will continue. The result of this will be an ever-diminishing group of what he calls 'core workers'. This consists of the professionals, technicians and managers, who will between them 'own' the organizational knowledge and run the show. They will be highly committed, work hard and long, and be rewarded with high salaries, fringe benefits and a guaranteed career structure. This 'core' will be complemented by 'contract workers', self-employed individuals, or companies who operate outside the parent organization, and who offer a service for the non-essential, specialized or routine work required by the 'core'. The vast majority of us, unless we choose to act now, will make up this third category – the 'flexible labour force'. This is the group from which the organizational 'core' will draw in times of need, and will consist, in the main, of part-time temporary workers.

As a freelance consultant, I am already a member of the ever-growing group of 'contract workers', many of whom are women, milling around the periphery of organizational life. According to Charles Handy this is not surprising:

> Women have often been less attracted to the 'inside' of organizations, if only because they had been made singularly unwelcome there. Women also, perforce, have to live extraordinarily flexible lives, juggling portfolios of work, family and community.[4]

Such contract/portfolio workers need to become 'self-managers of their own assets'[5] that is, to be clear about their skills, strengths and qualities, and to display a willingness to work on any areas of weakness via self-directed learning, training, supportive networks, counselling or therapy.

Portfolio people need to develop a product, skill or service and to assemble a portfolio that illustrates these assets. They must then go out and find their customers. Daunting stuff for many of us who may have only recently acquired confidence in our ability to survive organizational life; we are now being asked to consider operating *outside* of this framework! However, it is to our advantage to act now, for Handy believes, 'Organizational employment will be ending sooner rather than later for all of us'.[6]

So if Charles Handy is right, and organizations will be made up of these three different groups of workers, what is the likely impact on women and their place in the workforce? What strikes me, immediately, is that women have to be far more definite about what they want from their lives, and the role that work will play. Men have always assumed that paid work will be the most important aspect of their lives; do women want this for themselves too? Do you want to be a 'core' worker with all the sacrifices that will be involved, or would you prefer the flexibility, but inherent vulnerability, of one of the other two positions? I have already made the choice, and whilst some may appreciate the freedom this work pattern provides, others may find the lack of structure and guaranteed income inhibiting. Whatever your feelings, it is important for us all to stop and think about what we want, particularly if we are about to enter or re-enter the labour market, as the decisions we make will have a profound impact on our ability to make choices in the future. A lack of commitment to career goals now may close down the option of ever becoming a 'core' or a 'portfolio' worker.

THE INDIVIDUAL AND CHANGE

The key concepts we shall work with in this book are individual responsibility and change. Organizations and places of work are changing, and we need to react accordingly. According to Tom Peters:

> Today, organizations need to learn to love change, to love tumult, to love chaos — this is a prerequisite of organizational survival, let alone success.[7]

At the same time organizations are also being required to understand and appreciate the needs of their employees as well as their customers, and there is a growing awareness of the importance of customer care. Sir John Harvey Jones has highlighted the need for fair treatment of employees:

> Increasingly companies will only survive if they meet the needs of the individuals who serve in them; not just the question of payment, important as this may be, but people's true inner needs, which they may even be reluctant to express themselves.[8]

If chief executives and senior managers are really prepared to accept the wisdom of these highly respected individuals, women in paid employment will really benefit. Up until now work has very much been a male perserve, and even successful women like Anita Roddick testify to the difficulties many have had to tolerate; she claims that corporations are largely created by men, for men, and are frequently influenced by military or public-school models.

Hierarchical structures built on authority remain unchanged; many men cannot accept the rise of women to top management positions. This could be because they have never learned to deal with women other than as secretaries, wives, girlfriends, mothers or adjuncts to themselves.[9]

So what *are* our options for the future? Unless we all want to join the ranks of the contract/portfolio workers immediately, or set up our own organizations, we need to learn how to cope with men, while they struggle to learn how to cope with us! 'The process of gender socialization is a "culture trap" . . . which women are relatively ill-prepared for in organizational life . . . and men relatively ill-prepared to accept them.' We need to decide if and how we might need to change to adapt to the new world of work, whilst at the same time holding on to the values which we hold dear. We must take responsibility for our actions and their consequences, either in terms of limiting ourselves and our potential or, on a grander scale, polluting the environment. It won't be easy, but it is reassuring to remember the words of Margaret Mead:

> Never doubt that a small group of thoughtful, committed citizens can change the world. Indeed it is the only thing that ever has.

So what are your choices? What kind of future do you want for yourself? How might these choices impact on others and what are the likely consequences for our environment and the planet as a whole?

WORKING RELATIONSHIPS

Although the main skills required for coping with the changing nature of work and our relationship to it are assertion, time and stress management (ATS), a great deal of space in this book is given over to exploring working relationships with men, managing sexuality at work, dealing with sexual harassment, coping with the menopause, life and career planning and working with environmental issues. Organizational life seems to have provided an arena for male energy to forge ahead, unrestrained by female values. According to Judi Marshall,[10] these are as follows:

Female values	Male values
interdependence	separation
co-operation	control
receptivity	competition
merging	focused perception
acceptance	rationality
awareness of patterns	analysis
wholes and contexts	clarity
emotional tone	discrimination
being	activity
intuition	
synthesizing	

What is sad is the extent to which female values have been negated in our organizational life, and Marshall talks about the 'socially muted female principle',[11] whereby women and their values have been silenced. She goes on to say:

> Male–positive, female–negative is such a pervasive aspect of our Western public culture that it is unusual to identify ways in which women differ from men without the assumption being made that women are somehow inferior. Female characteristics and values, such as emotions, intuition and interdependence, are denied legitimacy, and are covertly or actively suppressed.[12]

Perhaps it is time for women to assert themselves in the workplace; to start saying what they need to say, and thus create a better sense of balance at work. With this in mind, one of the key themes throughout this book will be how to encourage women to find their voice in any organization, that is to have the confidence to articulate their perceptions, values and feelings. It reflects my struggle to learn how to achieve this, working as a female consultant within a variety of organizational settings, including the Health Service, local government, large private multi-nationals, and voluntary sector organizations. Men have a habit of defining reality for women. It takes a lot of courage to say, 'Well, actually, that's not true for me' or 'No, I don't think that is right!' Some men are so unused to being contradicted or gently challenged by 'a mere woman' that they tend to over-react and become unduly defensive.

At such times it is easy to be submerged by our inbuilt notions of acceptable female behaviour – 'nice girls don't have opinions' – rather than continue to say what we need to say. Sadly, many organizations lose the opportunity of hearing the voice of half the population. An interesting notion from Transactional Analysis is that we all have tapes or scripts running in our heads, recorded in early childhood, which reinforce certain behaviours. Women may hold a number of inappropriate tapes which discourage responsible actions. Taking the plunge and saying what you need to say may not make you popular in the first instance, but it will help you take charge of your life and future. This needs to be tempered by an awareness of organizational politics — by which I mean an understanding of how things may need to be said so that they will be heard — rather than individual woman being ignored or punished by the organizational culture. Women do have rights, as people and as workers. This book will help you identify those rights, and give you some skills in standing up for them in a variety of situations.

I have had to challenge some of my own tapes by daring to make public my thoughts about organizational life. As a result, I feel I have moved somewhat closer to finding my voice in an organizational setting. I hope, therefore, that this publication will help other women to find theirs, and thus increase their determination to speak out in the workplace. If this happens, then the 1990s will represent the decade in which women finally get what they deserve; their personal, political and organizational power.

An Introduction to the ATS Model

ATS (Assertion, Time and Stress Management) represents a set of skills and techniques to enable women to stand up for themselves and their rights in the workplace, whether they are working within a business or from home. In order to confront what may be out-dated notions of acceptable female behaviour, both from our own 'internalized tapes' and from the workplace, we need to know what our rights are, and how we might defend them. For instance, one of the tapes we may carry around in our heads is that we should always put other people's needs before our own. While this is a very fine sentiment, in practice it is unrealistic and unhelpful. There will always be times when this is appropriate, but there will also be occasions when we must put our own needs first. At the very least we need to be able to negotiate from a position of knowing what we would ideally like.

Having worked with women in organizations for many years, either as a trainer or as a consultant, I have come to the conclusion that these three skill areas of assertion, time management and stress management provide the basic stepping stones for women's development at work. Traditionally, women have not been encouraged to value or assert themselves, to protect their time, or to look after their own emotional or physical well-being. Unless we begin to recognize the importance of making these shifts in our behaviour, we will reinforce quite negative stereotypes about women, and we will never succeed in learning how to stand up for our rights.

In particular we need to:

* Know how to assert ourselves and our thoughts, values and opinions when necessary.

* Manage our time in relation to the key tasks and processes we are involved in.

* Manage our stress in relation to the pressures at work and home.

Effective stress management in particular is the key to surviving the organizational changes occurring at present. We are surrounded by businesses shedding staff, slimming down operational processes, focusing on cost-cutting exercises, and making employees more accountable. Whatever our line of work, we can confidently predict that such changes will create uncertainty, resulting in stress. In order to manage our stress effectively we must learn how to manage our time; and in order to do this we need to be able to assert ourselves. For example, if you are feeling stressed because you never seem to be able to get on top of your workload, you may need to manage your time more efficiently by defining your key tasks and priorities. You must then protect your decisions by saying no to unreasonable requests, or using the technique of broken record, (see page 20).

In this way ATS is a circular, rather than a linear, model, with one set of skills and behaviour feeding into another. Each is dependent upon the other; without one, the others fail. This is rather like life itself: sadly, we seem to have forgotten this, and employees are encouraged to see their responsibility solely in terms of securing the goals of the organization rather then ensuring the well-being of humanity and the world.

> A healthy life is dependent upon a healthy environment – that humans exist in a symbiotic relationship with the earth – and that to disregard this is destructive to us and the planet.[1]

WORKING TOWARDS POSITIVE CHANGE

Organizational survival in the 1990s will rely largely on the creation of a greater sense of balance within any organization. This could mean bringing in and appreciating the heart as well as the intellect, intuition as well as the logical approach, and valuing the process by which a task is achieved as well as its completion. In the short term, working women may have to bear some of the responsibility for creating a more person-centred work culture, where the whole person is valued. It may be time at last for 'rational man' to disappear, and for 'whole persons' to make their entry into the workplace. Women can help in this process by refusing to deny their essential humanity, and by standing up for the values they hold dear, such as co-operation and good interpersonal relationships. One of the ways we can do this is by showing our competence in relation to ATS, thus gaining credibility within the existing culture. We can model assertive, co-operative behaviour in a culture which tends to value competitive behaviour and male 'drive' or aggression. Having proved that we can manage this culture on our terms, our voices will be heard, our values considered, and eventually the culture will change, thus benefitting men, women and the world.

1

ATS – Assertion

Assertion – the ability to assert yourself, to say what you need to – is at the forefront of the ATS model. It is a vital key to managing our lives, abilities and relationships more effectively.

Why should it be so important for women to assert themselves at work? Well, because the world of work provides an arena in which certain male values and behaviours predominate so powerfully that many women feel they have either to conform to the stereotype of the non-assertive woman, or to become a pseudo male in order to get noticed. According to Gareth Morgan in *Images of Organization*:

> Many organizations are dominated by gender-related values that bias organizational life in favour of one sex over another. Thus ... organizations often segment opportunity structures and job markets in ways that enable men to achieve positions of prestige and power more easily than women ...[1]

ASSERTION OF RIGHTS

Is it possible to operate in a different way, and to uphold the values and behaviour women relate to, such as co-operation and good interpersonal relationships? If women could be more assertive at work it is likely that female values would begin to be appreciated too. Being assertive might mean contradicting false assumptions about women's value and worth; it would certainly involve challenging unacceptable behaviour from colleagues. But if approximately 40 per cent of the labour force is female, shouldn't women be starting to feel capable of asserting their rights more forcibly?

Maybe one of the reasons why this is not happening is the relative powerlessness of women in organizational terms. Not only do the vast majority work in the service industries, most at present are also destined to remain low in the hierarchy. Even though some women are entering managerial, administrative and professional occupations, very few achieve any real power: 'women tend to occupy the by-ways of the professions rather than the mainstream: they dominate in the back-up, services areas rather than the powerhouses'.[2]

So how does it feel to be destined for the service area rather than the powerhouse, a part of the 'flexible labour force' rather than one of the 'core'? Do you want to spend your life servicing the needs of others, or would you like a greater say in your own destiny and the culture of organizational life? The chance should be yours. Becoming more assertive could help you to achieve the life you want for yourself.

Obstacles to overcome

What prevents women from going for what they want at work? Other writers have documented the extent to which organizations are patriarchal in nature, giving some men power over other men, and all men power over women. The pyramid power structure in most organizations reflects this, and therefore women tend not to be valued within these institutions. Unfortunately, this reality is matched by women's limited sense of their own self-worth, which is hardly surprising given the messages many young girls receive about their value via the process of socialization. This will be discussed more fully later, but for the present it is important to acknowledge that women often suffer from feelings of low self-esteem, and have difficulty in establishing sufficient confidence in their abilities and skills to feel comfortable at work.

So what are women supposed to be like? The female stereotype is soft, loving, attentive, intuitive, afraid of achievement, poor at quantitative analysis, unable to make tough decisions, emotional, irrational and subjective. In contrast men are viewed as independent, objective, task-orientated, aggressive, good at problem-solving and decision-making. Men are seen to have the important skills and qualities; women are seen as lacking in some way.

The message organizations have been giving to women for a long time is that they need to suppress their feminine side, and develop more 'appropriate' male characteristics. Thus women who have succeeded in climbing the career ladder have tended to deny their femininity and played according to the male rules. Some have become 'armoured Amazons'[3], taking on board a defensive shell of male characteristics and behaviour. This is too high a price to pay, for it is destructive to women's psyche and, in the end, nothing changes because the male principle and male behaviour is reinforced by female modelling.

We all suffer if the feminine principle is denied; ourselves, our organizations and our planet. Another, healthier, way, is for women to assert their rights to be women within an organizational context. If women were able to challenge negative assumptions about themselves and the feminine, the repercussions could be enormous. Women would start to feel better about themselves; their confidence would improve, which in turn would affect their performance at work; they would begin to respect themselves, and thus gain the respect of others. The overall result would be more balanced individuals, and more balanced organizations.

ASSERTION IN PRACTICE

So what is assertion, and how might it help in this process of individual and organizational transformation? According to Anni Townsend[4] it means

1. Respecting myself, that is who I am and what I do.
2. Taking responsibility for myself, that is for how I feel and what I think and do.
3. Recognizing my own needs and wants independently of others, that is separate from what is expected of me in particular roles such as 'wife', 'partner', 'daughter'.
4. Making clear 'I' statements about how I feel and what I think.
5. Allowing myself to make mistakes, that is recognizing that sometime I will make a mistake and that it is OK to make mistakes.
6. Allowing myself to enjoy my successes, that is validating myself and what I have done, and sharing it with others.
7. Changing my mind, if and when I choose to.
8. Asking for 'thinking-it-over' time.

9. Asking for what I want, rather than hoping someone will notice what I want, and moaning later that I didn't get what I wanted.
10. Setting clear boundaries.
11. Recognizing that I have a responsibility towards others, rather than being responsible for others.
12. Respecting other people and their right to be assertive.

Doubts and guilt feelings

Quite an impressive list, and on first reading some women might think it sounds quite selfish, and thus unacceptable. After all, haven't we been taught that we shouldn't be selfish? One of our worst fears could be that others won't like us if we start to ask for what we want, celebrate our successes or admit to being competent. Many women's socialization does not provide them with an adequate sense of their own worth, and so other people's opinions are important as a measure of who and what they are. Thus women tend to be very dependent on the approval of others, and feel guilty if they don't live up to other people's expectations. How else would we accept the situation where most of us actually have two jobs, one in paid employment, the other managing at home?

Having been involved in women's training for over a decade, one of the consistent themes I have encountered in any discussion on assertion is the overwhelming sense of guilt that women have about the thought of standing up for themselves. Many of them really don't think they have rights in relation to others. They oppress themselves and their needs by believing they must always do what is right for everyone else, be this a family member, a friend or a colleague. It feels totally alien to them to decide what *they* might want from life.

This fact can work well for men, who will use it to their advantage. Some male managers will often employ charm to manipulate their female secretaries into working extra hard, and it is unlikely that they feel in the least bit guilty. It probably comes under the heading of 'a good management technique', making the best use of the resources available. On the other hand, I have met senior women staff who felt really guilty about asking their secretaries to do something that is legitimately within their role. Many men might view such behaviour as a display of weakness, but more often it displays the desire neither to manipulate nor exploit staff and to work from a position of integrity.

Knowing a little about assertion can help: the secretary can learn to stand up for her rights in relation to the unfair demands of her boss, and the female manager can assert her rights in relation to the tasks she needs her secretary to perform. The important concept in assertion is the notion of rights – your rights as an individual. Being assertive means standing up for your rights in such a way that you do not violate the rights of others. If you have certain rights then so do other people, independent of gender, race, sexual preference and disability.

Overcoming non-assertiveness and aggressiveness

In order to become more assertive we must question the process whereby we have been socialized into becoming acceptable young girls and women. In our childhood, the behaviour which was deemed appropriate was predominantly non-assertive. Young women were reinforced for behaviour which suggested they didn't have very strong feelings or wants. It was much more feminine to be coy, shy and demure, rather than asking for what you wanted and needed.

Non-assertive behaviour allows your rights to be violated, and there is a strong connection between this type of behaviour and depression. Women who can't assert themselves feel depressed a lot of the time because non-assertiveness leads to feelings of powerlessness and helplessness, and reinforces the sense of low self-esteem which more than likely prevents assertion in the first place. So women tend to comply with the needs of others, which suits most men in that non-assertive women fit in with their life/career plans. Organizations benefit too, by having a highly mobile workforce – the woman following upon the heels of her husband's next career move. No wonder women feel depressed!

Most women will be only too familiar with this pattern; they will certainly have seen it in their mothers, or close relatives and friends, if not in themselves. Assertion and being assertive is one way of breaking out of this negative cycle; it enables women to feel better about themselves and their potential to make things happen in the world. It allows women to feel more confident, and in charge of their lives.

Aggression in women, on the other hand, is often the flip side of non-assertion. Women who find it hard to assert themselves will, when frustrated, flip into aggression. As a result, they can be labelled as hysterical or unpredictable, or having a tendency to over-react to situations. They are seen to move from non-assertive into aggressive behaviour for no apparent reason, or rather for no reason that many men would easily understand.

What is not appreciated is the energy a woman may have been suppressing by not expressing her anger and frustration about a whole range of situations where she may have been ignored, devalued or undermined. Eventually it all proves too much for even the most demure and repressed of women and the rage bursts out, sometimes in a hurl of abuse and tears, covering the feelings of hurt and injustice she more than likely is also experiencing. Such behaviour is defined as aggressive because it violates the rights of others. Such extremes, however, could be prevented if women allowed themselves to admit to and express their anger more frequently. It is possible to do this assertively; you can tell someone they are making you angry as and when they do it, rather than having to lose control in order to discharge distress. Saying what needs to be said is important for our health, mental well-being and self-esteem. If we start to respect ourselves and our rights to speak out, others will start to respect us too.

And so, just to make sure the difference between the three modes of behaviour are clear, read through the following definitions from *Assertion Training*.[5]

Non-assertion means

* Having difficulty standing up for yourself.
  For example, staying behind to type a report for the boss when you had agreed to go swimming with a friend.

* Voluntarily relinquishing responsibility for yourself.
  For example, letting other people decide on what is best for you, such as your partner choosing the timing and location of your annual vacation.

* Inviting persecution by assuming the role of victim or martyr.
  For example, moaning constantly about having too much to do, and then letting your colleagues and boss dump more work on you.

Aggressive means

* Standing up for your rights in such a way that the rights of others are violated in the process.

    For example, demanding immediate attention and service from a staff member who is dealing with someone else.

* Being self-enhancing at the expense of putting down or humiliating others.

    For example, mocking a trainee who is having difficulty learning a task in which you are highly competent.

* Manipulation is an indirect form of aggression; it includes subterfuge, trickery, seduction and subtle forms of revenge.

    For example, pretending you care about a colleague, getting them to open up to you, and then using the information against them.

Assertiveness means

* Being able to express your needs, preferences, and feelings in a manner that is neither threatening nor punishing to others.

* Acting without undue fear or anxiety.

* Acting without violating the rights of others.

* Direct, honest communication between individuals interacting equally and taking responsibility for themselves.

Assertion is essentially about you, and how you use your power. If you act non-assertively you are giving your power away; if aggressively, you are using it to violate others; and if assertively, you are using it to say what you need and to negotiate for what you want.

If you have no previous knowledge of assertion, and no idea about how assertive you are, you may like to complete the following questionnaire to determine your strengths and weaknesses.

Assertiveness questionnaire

1. Do you generally express what you feel?
2. Do you find it difficult to make decisions?
3. Are you openly critical of others' ideas, opinions and behaviour?

4. Do you often avoid people or situations for fear of embarrassment?
5. Do you usually have confidence in your own judgement?
6. Do you insist that your spouse or flatmate takes on a fair share of household chores?
7. When a salesperson makes an effort, do you find it hard to say 'no', even when the merchandise is not really what you want?
8. Are you reluctant to speak up in discussion or debate?
9. If a person has borrowed something and is overdue in returning it, do you mention it?
10. Do you continue to pursue an argument after the other person has had enough?
11. When a person is unfair, do you say so?
12. Are you disturbed when someone watches you at work?
13. Do you find it difficult to maintain eye contact when talking to another person?
14. Do you complain in a restaurant when you don't get good service?
15. When you discover merchandise is faulty, do you return it?
16. Are you openly able to express love and affection?
17. Are you able to ask your friend for small favours of help?
18. Are you able to be open and frank in expressing both tender and angry feelings to men?

(Adapted from *Assertion Training* by D. Clarke and J. Underwood.)

So what has that revealed about yourself and your level of assertiveness? It might be helpful to get a friend to answer the questionnaire too, and see how you differ. Why do you think you find it hard to assert yourself in certain situations? Are you embarrassed at the thought of making a fuss? Would you rather put up with unsatisfactory service in a restaurant than risk an embarrassing situation with the waiter or owner? Are you worried about being made to look a fool? Whatever gets in the way, you can take comfort from the fact that you are not alone; it *is* possible to change, and assertion can help.

Understanding your rights

Women often find it difficult to assert themselves in particular situations because they are unaware of their rights. As already mentioned, the role of women in the past was to service the needs of others, and they must be careful that work does not become an extension of the 'mothering' role played within the family. A satisfying and rewarding time at work is not based on playing the martyr. Women need to learn how to stand up for themselves and be clear about the limits to their responsibility for others.

How about writing your own Bill of Rights, similar to the example outlined below? I have mentioned the concept of 'rights' a great deal, but what do you have a right to? As a woman, as an individual, as a worker, in all types of situations? If your mother wants you to come and visit, and you are totally exhausted from a hard week at work, do you have the right to say 'no'? If your boss wants you to work overtime and your spouse/partner wants you at home, what rights do you have? Write down your thoughts and feelings, starting with the line: 'I have the right to . . .' and see what comes into your head. Your own list of rights will provide some interesting ideas to think about, and will be a starting point for reflection and discussion.

To become more assertive, it is important to start developing an image of yourself as someone with rights, whatever you eventually decide those rights are. Acting assertively means being able to stand up for your rights and negotiate for what you want, when you need to.

Bill of Rights

As a woman I have the right to:

1. State my own wants and needs.
2. Set my own priorities.
3. Be treated with respect.
4. Be treated as intelligent and capable.
5. Express my feelings.
6. Express my opinions and values.
7. Say 'yes' and 'no' for myself.
8. Make mistakes.
9. Change my mind.
10. Express my uncertainty or confusion.
11. Decline responsibility for other people's problems.
12. Deal with others without being dependent upon them for approval.

(The above is modified from *A Woman In Your Own Right*, by Anne Dickson (Quartet Books)).

Having drawn up your own list, write it out and display it prominently, so that you reinforce your sense of someone with rights. In addition, it would certainly help to participate in a women-only assertion training course. Single gender groups can provide a forum within which women are able to share their issues and get support for their desired changes. It can be such a relief to have some space to talk about yourself, and the problems you may be having at home and at work. In addition, there is the opportunity of learning more about the techniques examined here, plus having the time to get feedback on your presentation and skills. Here are a number of techniques you can start putting into practice.

Broken Record

The goal is to be clear about what you want to say and to make this known without getting angry or irritated.

When it's useful: in conflict situations; when refusing unreasonable requests; when saying 'no'; when asking for clarification; when expressing feelings or opinions.

What you do: you speak as if you were a broken record. You need to be persistent, to stick to the point of what you want to say; you just keep saying it over and over again, ignoring all the side issues.

You don't respond to anything unrelated to the point you are making, or get caught up in arguments. Just say what you want to say, in a calm and repetitive voice, until the other person hears it.

The steps:
1. Identify your goal and make a clear statement.
    * 'I can't work this evening.'
    * 'I won't be able to get this work done by Friday.'
    * 'No, I can't cover for you next week.'

2. Ignore any statements which will cloud the issue.
    * 'But the point is . . .'
    * 'I don't think you heard me. I'm not able to work this evening.'
    * 'Let me say it again, I won't be able to stay behind this evening.'

3. Repeat your statement calmly as often as is necessary.

4. Ensure that your non-verbal language matches your verbal message. You need to look as if you mean what you are saying.

Broken Record is a very powerful technique. Although it might sound as though the person using it looks rather silly, she actually starts to feel and look increasingly confident as the interaction goes on. The key to this technique is having clarity about what you feel and want, and just sticking with it in the face of challenge, or even bullying. You just stay with your truth, rather than fitting in with others.

A situation where it can be very useful is when refusing a drink. If you are being pressurized to have a drink, think about using Broken Record. Such an encounter could go like this, from your side:

'No, I don't want a drink, but thank you.'
'No, I really don't want one.'
'Thanks for offering, but I really don't want another drink.'
'Honestly, that's very kind of you, but I really don't want a drink.'

Even the most determined bully would have to give up in the face of such assertion!

So, when do you think that Broken Record could be useful for you? When do you find yourself agreeing to things rather than saying what you really feel? How about trying Broken Record out next time someone puts pressure on you, maybe at work, or in a shop, and see what a difference it makes. Start off with a relatively easy situation. You could always ask a friend to do a small role-play with you, around refusing a drink or an invitation out, and see what modifications she suggests about your non-verbal communication (see page 27). Ask for feedback on facial expression, eye-contact and overall posture. Ask the question 'How assertive did I look and what improvement could I make?'

How to say 'No'

The next technique we will explore is being able to say 'No'. This is such a little word, and yet many women find it very hard to say when people make a request of them, preferring to make up all kinds of excuses. Is it because saying 'No' isn't nice, and so people won't like us? This seems to be true for lots of women; they want to please to such an extent that they can't bear to refuse any request, however unreasonable. As a result, they find themselves taking on more and more work, covering for other people, and having increased responsibility without recognition or reward. When was the last time you said 'No'? How did it make you feel, and why? What does that tell you about yourself?

If you have problems in this area, try role-playing short scenes with a friend in which she makes a request and you have to say 'No'. Think about typical demands such as, 'Could you get this work finished by coffee time?' or 'Can you pick up my dry-cleaning in your lunch hour?' Ask your friend to put pressure on you, to make you feel guilty about your refusal. Combine the 'No' with 'Broken Record'. Ask for feedback on how assertive your 'No' was, and any changes you may need to make to your non-verbal communication.

Here are some guidelines for saying 'No' effectively. When someone makes a request of you try the following:

* Notice your immediate reaction and trust it.

* Give yourself time: at the slightest sign of hesitation in yourself try saying: 'I don't know. I need some more information.'

* Practise saying 'No' without excessive apology or excuses. You can avoid any feelings of guilt by remembering you are refusing the request, not the person.

* Make sure you do say the word 'No'. Many of us imagine we have made a refusal and in reality that word has not appeared in our statement.

* Check that your body language is also saying 'No', without apology or aggression.

* Practise saying 'No' often and aloud when you are on your own.

* Try easy situations first, and save the more difficult ones until you can build on success.

Asking for time

Another important technique is being able to give yourself time to think about a request that is being made of you. We are often asked to do something when our minds are preoccupied with another task or activity. Instead of agreeing to the demand, and taking the easy way out, it is best to ask for time to consider the request and say when we will let the person know of our decision. This then gives us the thinking space to:

* Consider the request.
* Weigh up the pros and cons.
* Determine the likely consequences of agreeing or refusing, both in the short term and the long term.
* Consider the impact of either decision on our relationship with the other person.

Having taken the time we need, we feel in a better position to make a decision. If we say 'Yes' after much consideration we cannot play the martyr at a later stage; we knew what we were doing when we accepted the request. Similarly, if we say 'No', we must do so in the knowledge of the likely consequences, and not moan about them later.

What sort of request would it help you to make if you asked for 'thinking-it-over time'? What have you regretted agreeing to recently? If you had given yourself time to reflect would you have decided to say 'No'? This is a powerful technique. Give yourself the permission to use it.

When to ask for time
When people make a request, give orders/directions, or ask a favour, and you are not totally clear about how you wish to respond. It is important to let yourself think about the implications of what is being asked. Clarify the pros and cons and reach the decision which makes sense for you.

What to do
1. Listen carefully to the request/order/favour.
2. Make sure you understand what is being asked of you.
3. Pause, take a breath and think about what is being requested.
4. Acknowledge that you understood what has been said and the feelings of the other person.
5. Say, 'I can't decide now, I need time to think about it.'
6. Specify the amount of time needed and how you will notify the person about your decision, for example by phone, by visit, by letter; in five minutes, one hour, tomorrow, next week, and so on.
7. Make sure that you get back to that person with your decision in the agreed time.

This is quite a simple technique, yet it will save you a lot of heartache. It is much more responsible to be clear in your communications with others. If you can't do what is being requested, say so now; don't keep people hanging around. Some people actually say 'Yes' when they mean 'No', and they manifest the 'No' by not actually doing what was requested. They never really had any intention of doing anything, but didn't have the courage to say 'No'. Think what difficulties such individuals create for themselves and the organizations they work for! It may not be easy to say 'No', but the amount of discomfort you experience in the short term will far outweigh that caused by taking on something you either can't or won't do.

Disarming anger

If you stop doing what other people want, or are unable to meet their needs, you may find that they start getting angry with you. This may involve a family member, someone at work, or a customer using the services provided by your organization. When this happens, you can use the technique known as Disarming Anger, by which you reduce the anger of the other person. Most of us dislike people being angry with us, but women in particular seem to find it especially distressing. Being comfortable with this technique should give you the confidence to deal with the anger, rather than running away from it or retreating into hurt feelings and tears.

When you have read through the technique, think about situations in which you have to deal with others' anger, and see if this would make a difference.

The goal
When you are faced with a situation in which someone is angry, you use the technique to reduce the feelings of anger so that:

1. You feel more comfortable.
2. You can begin to listen.
3. You can begin to solve the problem together.

When to use it
When someone is telling you off or is involved in a personal tirade against you. This might be a boss, friend, parent, someone you live with, or an authority figure.

What you do

1. Recognize the anger you are picking up.
   * 'Okay, I can see that you are very angry.'

2. Express your desire to solve the problem actively.
   * 'I want to hear what you have to say. Let's try and work this out together.'

3. Get the angry person to lower his/her voice and sit down, using a normal voice and calming approach.
   * 'Let's sit down and have a chat about what's happening.'

4. Use active listening to hear all the complaints before moving on to problem-solving.
   * 'I can see that this has been bothering you for a long time.'
   * 'This must have seemed like the last straw.'

It often helps to admit early on the possibility that you might have been part of the problem.

* 'You're right, maybe I could have arrived a bit earlier.'
* 'Perhaps I did make a mistake.'

This way of approaching anger assumes you are willing to handle the problem and move beyond active listening to trying to resolve the conflict.

So what do you think? Do you think you could use it? Many women deal with the public in their work, for example in shops and offices, at the reception desk, as nurses, social workers or sales staff. Customers often vent their anger on these front-line workers, because they are the nearest to hand. There are courses designed for 'Coping with aggression', and it might be worth attending one if you have noticed increased incidents of aggression from consumers. Using the above technique is a useful first step, however, and could prevent the situation from escalating into an aggressive incident.

Positive and negative assertion

How easy do you find it to accept a compliment or to receive criticism? Many women find it difficult to receive any feedback on their behaviour because of their low self-esteem, and in case it confirms their worst fears that they are incompetent in some way. Assertive behaviour involves being open to receiving and giving as much feedback as possible. Feedback can be seen as a 'gift'; it provides individuals with information of which they may have been unaware; it makes change possible. You can choose to act on this gift and change your behaviour, or you can ignore it – it's up to you.

Being assertive means having the courage to give feedback to others. Unless you tell people what it is they are doing, or not doing, which upsets you, how will they ever be able to change their behaviour? So if you are not happy with the actions of a family member, friend or colleague, give them some feedback on it.

Positive assertion

Helps you to accept genuine compliments.

What you do

You just agree in a simple, direct way.

* 'Thank you, I think this dress looks good on me too.'
* 'Thank you, I really felt good about the way I handled that customer too.'

Negative assertion

To cope and to keep your dignity when you are criticized for making a mistake which there is no doubt you have made.

What you do

You accept assertively those things that are negative about yourself.

In the simplest manner you cope verbally with your errors, as if they are exactly that, no more or no less. Remember: errors are just errors; mistakes are just mistakes.

Giving and receiving feedback

Giving feedback

It is appropriate to give honest, direct feedback to another person when you think their behaviour is inappropriate to the situation. Remember also to give positive feedback where praise is due.

* Feedback is information to the other person about how their behaviour affects you.

* You own your thoughts, feelings and opinions by making 'I' statements (rather than 'You' statements).
* You speak directly to the other person (rather than complaining about them to others).
* You comment on the behaviour, not the person.
* You are specific in your comments.
* You can conclude by saying what behaviour you would prefer.

Receiving feedback

When you are receiving either positive or negative feedback, do not let your feelings hinder the use of the important information which is being offered to you.

* Listen without comment until the other person has finished speaking.
* Accept compliments assertively — own your strengths.
* If the feedback is 'loaded' in some way, express your feelings about the statement: 'I feel angry/upset when you say that'.
* Ask for comment on your behaviour rather than on your personality.
* If feedback is vague, ask the speaker to be more specific. 'What exactly was it about my behaviour in the situation which you liked/disliked?'
* Do not swallow criticism whole: look for consistent feedback from a number of people first. Take responsibility for which aspects of the feedback you will act on — it is your choice to change your behaviour.

Non-verbal communication

It is important that your body language complies with your statement. Words are only a small part of communication, and the body speaks volumes. Does your body language help or hinder your powers of communication? Stand in front of a mirror, and imagine you are acting assertively. What impression is your body making? For instance, do you have a tendency to slouch, stand off-balance, wring your hands? If so, what messages would you be giving out about your confidence level? Do you manage to maintain eye contact with others when you are talking with them? If not, what impact do you have? Do you have any idea of your typical facial expressions? If not, the first step is to ask for some information from family members, friends and colleagues at work. If you have access to a video, even better. Run through a scene with a friend where you are trying out one of the techniques identified above, and focus the camera on your facial expressions and body movements during the whole interaction.

Posture

Seeing oneself on video is a sobering experience, but once again it is a gift: this is how others see you. If can feel a little bit like going to the dentist; you feel better after the initial shock and discomfort! If you don't like the impression you are giving, remember that here is another opportunity for change and development. If you discover you have bad posture, you could consider having massage to release tension stored in the body, practising yoga, or attending a keep-fit or aerobics class.

The Alexander Technique, covered more fully in the section on stress management (p. 67), is another way of improving your posture. It is a method for helping us to 'unlearn' the bad postural habits we have picked up over the years. A young baby has wonderful posture; but look at any schoolchild and you will notice the start of bad postural habits. Sitting at a desk, or at the wheel of a car, or slouched in front of the television, does nothing for us. So, even though taking Alexander classes may be rather more expensive and time-consuming than you had considered, your back will appreciate the experience. You will see the benefits in terms of how much more confident you appear, and you may well prevent chronic backache in the years to come. Alternatively, you may like to consider dance or Tai Chi classes if you have a sense of being 'ungrounded' or not have a very solid presence in the world.

Eye-contact

Next, think about your eye-contact. This is the most significant aspect of non-verbal communication to the sighted. Aim for a steady, relaxed contact, rather than an intrusive stare or a shifting gaze. The first can suggest an aggressive stance; the latter, non-assertion.

Speaking voice

What does your voice sound like? Is it strong and assertive, or timid and breathless? Practising deep breathing and voice projection will help. You might like to consider attending a voice workshop, where you will be given help and techniques to 'own your voice'. Are any of your gestures especially irritating? Get feedback, and see if you need to modify or eliminate any.

Remember, the impression you make on others will depend to a large extent on your non-verbal communication, if you want to come across as more assertive you must match your words with your body language.

The assertive woman

* Uses good eye-contact.
* Has control over volume, tone, rate and quality of voice.
* Has an expressive face which matches what is being said.
* Is aware of posture, and projects an assertive stance.
* Has a style of dress which adds to her confidence.

Other important concepts to consider are 'personal space', and the role of smiling in assertive behaviour.

Research suggests that men tend to maintain a larger 'personal space' than women, who allow their space to be invaded. Men will also use space as their own, for instance sprawling out, sitting with their legs and arms extended during discussions with others. Women, however, tend to keep their limbs close to their body. Not taking space suggests a lack of assertion. It might be useful to monitor what happens when you change your habitual response to space. Does it make you feel more powerful to define your territory more assertively? Do others respect this, and therefore you?

Women have been observed to smile and giggle more than men when in conversation. Frequent and inappropriate smiling is associated with non-assertive behaviour. Again, monitor yourself to see if you need to modify your behaviour.

Before we go on to explore the time and stress management, it might be helpful to identify a process that you will find helpful when assertively confronting a situation. This is known as the *assertive script* and consists of five points to consider prior to dealing with any communication problem you may be having.

The assertive script

If you know that you are about to confront someone, and need to be assertive, plan out the following scene.

Describe. . . the situation as you see it.
Express. . . how you feel about the situation.
Empathize. . . recognize the other person's situation, point of view.
Specify. . . what it is you would like to be different.
Choose. . . indicate the choices you see open to you resulting from the other's response to your request.

An example of the above could be as follows:

1. I've been thinking about how much time we spend chatting at work, and how this means I often feel under pressure to finish my work.
2. While I really enjoy talking with you, I'm feeling quite worn out by rushing at the end of the day.
3. I know you are so familiar with the work that it doesn't present you with too many challenges any more, but that isn't the case for me.
4. What I would like is an agreement that we limit our conversations to certain parts of the day.
5. If we had this agreement, I would feel able to relax and enjoy our time together, and get my work completed.

Would you find this technique helpful? It does not imply that you should become word perfect before an encounter, but it should give an overview of what it is you want to say so that you can cope with any anxiety you experience during the interaction.

These techniques should provide you with enough material to practise being more assertive in your life. However, reading about assertion is no substitute for attending a course where you will get support from others. Check out what is available locally, as many colleges and extra-mural departments run events at reasonable prices. These can be evening classes or day schools.

Before we move on it might be fun to see what you make of the following exercises. Complete the scenes outlined below, and see where you might have problems asserting yourself. Suggest non-assertive, aggressive and assertive responses to the following.

1. A close friend, who knows you are going to be away for a week, asks if she can borrow your car. You like her very much,

but don't know what sort of a driver she is. Give an example of one of each of the following: non-assertive; aggressive; assertive.

2. You are a member of a training course in which the men are patronizing the women. One of the men turns to you and says, 'Well, dear, now what was it you were saying?' You reply in one of three ways: non-assertive; aggressive; assertive.

3. Your child is sick. Both you and your partner work full-time. Your partner says he must go to work. You reply in one of the following ways: non-assertive, aggressive; assertive.

4. You are at the cinema. The person next to you is smoking and you find this very annoying and distracting. When lighting yet another cigarette he/she says: 'You don't mind if I smoke, do you?'. You reply: non-assertive; aggressive; assertive.

5. You have been asked to take on some different, but boring, work. There have been hints that co-operative people 'get on' in your organization. You deal with the situation by saying one of the following: non-assertive; aggressive; assertive.

6. You have been in your job a year, but find that it does not provide you with the experiences you were promised. You respond in one of the following ways: non-assertive; aggressive; assertive.

(Source: Career-life planning workshops for Women Managers: Bristol Polytechnic/MSC.)

So, is there any improvement on the original assertion questionnaire? Do you feel more confident about knowing how to assert yourself in certain situations? Don't worry if you still feel a little overwhelmed by the implications of a more assertive you; go at the pace that seems best for you, and take as much time as you need, but don't forget that you have the right to assert yourself, even if it makes you and others uncomfortable in the short term. The rewards for you, and them, will be enormous in the longer term.

Now lets move on to time management. As you start to read through the next chapter you will see how closely time management is related to assertion. So if you want to use the time available more appropriately develop your ability to assert yourself.

2

ATS – Time Management

Time management is the second strand to the ATS model. Having started to explore who we are, and what we might want, via assertion, time management consists of a range of skills and techniques to help us protect one of our most valuable resources – our time.

LEARNING TO VALUE OUR TIME

When we were growing up it is unlikely that many of us were actively encouraged to identify what we wanted from life, or to understand how important it was to value and protect the time available to us. As little girls we were encouraged to worry more about our appearance, and making ourselves look pretty, than with how we might make the best use of our allotted three score years and ten! On the other hand we learnt that other people's time *was* important; if not our mother's, then most certainly our father's. Whilst men's time was important, ours was not. Thus our time could be invaded, interrupted and wasted, and we were expected to fit in with the arrangements of others without prior consultation.

Years of conditioning mean that we have not been taught to take our time and space seriously, and we don't really know how to protect it from misuse. Thus we can end up letting our partner and children determine how our time is spent at home, and allow others to abuse it at work. If, for instance, we have a boss who is a bad time manager, we may end up not only having to sort him out, but to constantly work against the clock to meet deadlines he has mismanaged. This was a common problem for the secretarial and administrative staff of a small unit where I was once employed.

The men were always dumping a load of work on them at the last minute and expecting miracles. Unfortunately the women were so competent they invariably managed the impossible! Whilst admiring their skill and efficiency, it upset me to see such abuse, and because the women so rarely complained the men never realized the extent of their arrogance and the insensitivity of their behaviour.

It is interesting to note in this context that sexual harassment can be seen as an extension of the assumptions that many men have about their 'rights' to invade women's space and time. It has been defined as:

> ... unwanted and intrusive male behavour, of whatever kind forced on women ... whether it's in the form of un-wanted sexual advances or demands for time, attention and sympathy...[1]

Some men make enormous demands on women's time, and yet don't seem to appreciate what has been offered. It often feels as though the support some women offer is so much taken for granted that it is in some way invisible, with no understanding of the cost to the individuals concerned. For instance, many of the support staff previously mentioned would get emotionally and physically ground down by the constant demands of the male staff. When important deadlines had to be met they would work all hours, and yet this generosity and professionalism was rarely acknowledged. It was just assumed the women would put them-selves out. Any women who complained was seen as over-reacting, or in need of further training, or uncommitted to the organizational goals.

In contrast men *are* seen as being committed to these goals. For a start they are rewarded more, both in terms of status and income, and they have the space and time to devote to their careers. Most, if not all, have support at home, wives looking after the nitty gritty of daily life so, unlike their secretaries, they do not have to cater for the emotional and physical demands of dependants. No wonder women can experience more stress at work; they have two full-time jobs. Where is their space and time? I know of a number of women colleagues who have to resort to the bathroom to get some time alone, and even then can't always be sure this space will be respected.

Perhaps such assumptions and behaviour are related to patterns in the family, in that boys sometimes seem to feel they have the right to invade their mother's space, and demand her time and attention, in a way that in the past has been unthinkable in relation to their fathers. Perhaps a boy would demand more of his father if he were at home more. The concept of 'absent father', the father who is rarely home because he is out at work, is interesting to consider here. It is probable that boys also yearn for the attention and approval of their fathers, but have to make do with their mothers, who are more often available. Certainly, men seem to accept and expect organizational life to demand they prove themselves worthy of the respect of other men, the boss/father figure, whereas they don't feel the need to earn the respect of the women at work. They tend to take women for granted, and assume women will fit in with their needs, rather than the other way round.

PROTECTING OUR TIME

As the tendency to misuse our time is so familiar, it is difficult for women at work to recognize how they might be colluding with a potentially abusive relationship. After all, if we are supposed to look after the needs of others, doesn't that include men at work too? What we may see as caring and supportive behaviour, however, may be interpreted as weakness and inappropriate sensitivity. Most women know how important it is to make time for others. We understand and appreciate the importance of interpersonal relationships, yet we may also need to protect this generosity of spirit from misuse by others.

The majority of women know how to be good listeners; we can empathize, show concern and warmth. But this uses energy and time which we could sometimes spend more appropriately on ourselves and our needs as workers. It is essential, therefore, that we balance our concern for others with a sense of our own needs for time and space. This will be covered more fully in the stress management chapter, but it is worth noting here that while it is important to value others' time, we also need to learn how to protect our own time from the demands of others.

I have allowed colleagues to misuse my time in the past. When I worked for a voluntary sector organization, my male colleague would spend hours recounting amusing experiences in his personal life, which meant I didn't get on with what I wanted to do. Because

I liked him, and didn't want to appear rude and unfriendly, I never challenged his misuse of my time, but I do remember feeling angry and frustrated. Not surprisingly, if he was busy, he was not prepared to spend time listening to me! Why didn't I confront this behaviour? I'm not sure, but I think I thought it was expected of me to be his willing audience. Again, perhaps this is a result of the socialization process: to assume oneself to be a member of the audience on life, rather than a prime actress. Men are the heroes who go off in search of adventure, while women wait at home for news of them – or that was what the myths and stories of the past suggested. We have more choice now, and by learning to protect our time, we can occasionally play the lead!

TACKLING GUILT AND LOW SELF-ESTEEM

During discussions on training events women always admit to feelings of immense guilt if they don't fit in with other people's needs and expectations. We are so used to others assuming they have the right to our time and attention that we may even feel guilty when we experience resentment. Why is this? Is it because our personal expectations are so high that we really think we have to live up to the image of the perfect wife/partner and mother? Do we really believe we need to be 'superwoman' to feel okay about ourselves? Do we value ourselves so little that we can't start to relax unless we are proving we are better than others? We are very tough on ourselves, and can create enormous stress by making such unrealistic demands. This will be explored more fully in the chapter on stress management, but it is important to bear in mind the strong relationship between high demands, bad time management and stress.

The unattainable stereotype

So what creates the low self-esteem, the guilt? One way of thinking about it may be via the theories of counselling psychology. Many counsellors would suggest that we have a sense of both the actual self, that is who we are, and an idealized self, which is the way we would ideally like to be. When the gap between the two is too great, we may suffer from a sense of personal inadequacy and failure. If this model is true, it would be very hard for women to feel good about themselves, as the stereotype is unattainable. After all, we are supposed to be soft, nurturing, passive, dependent, the perfect wife/partner, the perfect mother, the dutiful daughter, sexually attractive and available for our partner, an excellent cook, the ideal hostess, plus competent at our paid work as well. No one could achieve all this, and yet women try all the time to live up to these expectations. The whole package is a fantasy!

BEING OURSELVES

As women, we need to remember that we are all individuals with different strengths and weaknesses. We are okay the way we are. We may choose to improve on aspects of our behaviour, such as assertion, but having a weakness in something doesn't make us 'bad', or 'not okay'. As women, we need to become much more realistic about our expectations in life, and only by doing this will we be able to enjoy who we are and what we do. It is essential, therefore, to challenge the unrealistic 'idealized self', and to bring it closer to what we actually are. The idealized self provides us with a purpose, a sense of what we are working towards. However, this must be an achievable goal or we will sink into despair about our perceived inadequacy.

Starting to improve our self-esteem means beginning to value ourselves, becoming more assertive, and learning to protect our time from misuse. We need to become clearer about what it is we want from life (see Chapter 4) but we also need to know what it is we want to achieve on a day-to-day basis. Life/career planning is the overview; time management is the daily practice.

BALANCING OUR NEEDS AND OTHERS' NEEDS

How do we do this if we have always been encouraged to put the needs of others before our own? A good starting point is by asserting your rights, by 'saying No' and 'Asking for time'. Most of us would not choose to abdicate our responsibilities to others, but we need to strike a better balance between our needs and theirs. For instance, do we really need to be totally responsible for household chores and domestic detail? Couldn't some of these be shared out amongst other family members? How about your partner getting the weekly shop, and the children taking their share of the washing up and cleaning? What about buying in some help? How about having someone in to do the ironing? What a relief that could be! The choices are endless, and the potential rewards enormous.

A close friend, with a full-time job, young children and a busy partner, negotiated to pay someone to come in and cook a range of wholesome meals every week. These were then frozen and available for the evening meal. This took pressure off both her and her partner, and meant the whole family had quality time together at meal times. Prior to this arrangement, meal times had been rather fraught affairs. Remember, change needs to start with us; if we alter our assumptions and behaviour it can have a knock-on effect on others. We can liberate our lives, and others', we if learn to manage our time better and don't assume we are responsible for everything.

MAKING THE MOST OF OUR TIME

In essence, time management is about having greater awareness of the choices available, and the consequences of either acting or not acting on those choices. It is about taking responsibility for ourselves and our decisions, learning from our experiences and making the necessary adjustments. In order to manage our time better we need to take stock of how we are using/misusing it at present. In the back of our minds we need to hold a sense of what it is we really want to achieve in our life time. The section on life/career planning will help you to define your life goals. Having decided what is important in our lives, we then set ourselves key priorities, and identify ways of achieving these, maybe in consultation with others. We must be clear about what we want and where we are going.

Achieving ambitions

Say for example that one of your life goals is to have a well-paid, interesting job. What do you need to do to achieve this? You may have to get certain qualifications, or work experience. A lot of women are interested in management as a possible career option. What are the options available? To begin with you would need to start displaying management potential, and thus get noticed. At the same time you could attend some management training events, starting with the occasional one-day workshops, then moving on to a three- or four-day management courses. Another option is to enrol on a Diploma in Management Studies, or if you are really keen, apply to complete a MBA (Master's degree in Business Administration). You might need to decide, too, if you are going to approach your organization for funding, or pay for any training yourself. The options and decisions are endless, but merely dreaming about becoming a manager doesn't make it happen. You start with the dream, and then map out and work through the necessary steps towards achieving your goal.

Whenever we explore our own use of time we need to be sensitive to those patterns of behaviour which sabotage our best attempts at taking more control of our lives. For instance, you may want a well-paid job in your organization, but have such a persistent problem with time management that you are late for work most days. What does this pattern mean? What are you either saying about yourself, or saying to other people, by being a bad time-keeper? You may be giving the impression of not caring about your work, or conveying an image of sloppiness and inefficiency. Others may read it as a lack of concern for the needs of others — your colleagues and customers. However it is interpreted, it will have consequences for your reputation as a worker, and will thus effect any career bids you make. So if you want the well-paid job, you will either need to modify your attitude to punctuality, or buy a better alarm clock, or excel in other ways which counterbalance the persistent lateness. One thing is for certain — you will have to do something *positive*.

Sorting out priorities

So let's start with step number one: reviewing our responsibilities. We all have responsibilities, towards ourselves and others, but every so often we need to decide which still need our attention. For instance, parents have a responsibility for their children; but as the children get older, it is in their interests that the parents gradually let them have more control over their own lives. This is not to be confused with abdication of responsibility; the parents are working in the interests of the child, helping him or her approach adulthood. Getting the balance right is what makes adolescence such a trying time for parents and offspring alike.

At the same time we have responsibilities towards our parents; but does that mean we let them live our lives for us? We need to be able to negotiate, at times, for some limits to our involvement with them. We must learn how to deal with their sometimes manipulative behaviour without feeling overwhelmed by guilt.

So, what are the responsibilities you could shed, postpone or delegate? Let's start by listing all the things for which you feel responsible, and then prioritize these using the ABC system. This technique, and most of the others identified in this section, are taken from a book by Alan Lakein.[2]

'ABC'

In this system you prioritize by placing a capital letter A against all those items on the list that you consider really important, B for those you think are not quite so important, and C for those that are unimportant. Then eliminate the Bs by deciding whether they are either important, and thus an A, or unimportant and thus a C. You should then be left with a list of As and Cs. The best use of your time is to concentrate your energy on achieving the A responsibilities, or tasks. You do the Cs only if you have spare capacity. This technique is indicating very clearly that you don't have enough time to do everything, and therefore you must make some choices, based on the importance of a responsibility or task.

Let's examine the situation where a woman employee is faced with the choice of meeting her responsibility to her employer, by working the overtime she or he requires, or that of her partner, by being at home. Which is the A responsibility? I am sure it will be a different answer for all of us, but, having made the choice, we have to live with the consequences of our decision, and we must therefore be very clear which is most important and act accordingly. For instance, if you want to get on in your present job, you may decide the needs of the boss are an A priority. If you are going through a particularly difficult patch in your relationship with your partner, that may be the A priority. Remember to take the decision, and live with the consequences assertively.

Numbering the priorities

Another way of sorting out the priorities in your life is to number them in order of importance, as in A1, A2, A3, and so forth. This means that you would work at achieving A1 first, then move on to A2, and so on. An important concept related to the ABC method is that of the 'overwhelming A': the A task you know you need to do, yet somehow never quite find the time. Many people seem to be experts at accumulating 'overwhelming As'. The important report that needs to be written, the car service that needs to be arranged, the phone call to a potential customer. As time goes on, these tasks become even more onerous, and seem almost to have a presence of their own. They sit on our shoulders demanding attention, never letting us relax.

The Swiss cheese method

If you know that this tends to happen to you, try the Swiss cheese method to defeat procrastination. It works for me, and has helped a number of friends get to the end of what had become a mammoth task. Take the following steps:

* You get started on the task, even if you only have a few minutes of free time.

* You turn the task into a number of small jobs, thus making a series of small holes in it.

* You tell yourself that you only need to spend five minutes at most on the task, so it doesn't matter if you don't enjoy it.

* Once you've started, however, you will find that the task isn't as awful as you feared, and you can often find the energy to stay with it longer than originally intended.

In short, have a go at it, even if you only take a little bite, and feel free to stop when you want to.

Dealing with the minor problems

The Cs in your life can be dealt with when you have time and space for them. I know what mine are: the filing, non-essential phone-calls and administration, and my book-keeping. I know from past experience that if I don't put some time aside for them, these Cs can become 'overwhelming As'. The book-keeping, for example, only needs to be done once a month for me to feel in control of the mass of receipts and invoices. If for some reason I don't manage to do the books at the end of the month, I am loathe to get going. I convince myself that it will be horrendously difficult and time-consuming, and keep putting it off. Once I've started, however, often by using the Swiss cheese method, I'm delighted to find that I quite enjoy it, and certainly feel enormous satisfaction when it's done!

On the other hand, if I spent every day worrying about the book-keeping, and doing a little bit just to keep it under control, this could be a tremendous waste of time, It's not important in terms of my priorities, which are focused on the consultancy and training events I run. So don't worry about miscalculating the importance of something, and assigning it to the C list instead of the A; inevitably you will receive some feedback which will enable you to rectify the situation. Just keep reminding yourself that you can't do it all; decide what's most important, and get on and do it.

Try not to let the system slip when you are under pressure, because that is when you need it most. I have noticed how easy it is to focus on C activities when this happens. I feel better because I am getting things done, but unfortunately those tasks are not very important. So watch yourself and keep asking 'What is the best use of my time right now?' Should you really be doing the filing, when there is that important (but difficult) letter to write? Why are you settling down to catch up with some non-essential administration, when you promised to phone that new customer? Keep reminding yourself of the need to prioritize, and you will become a better time manager.

COPING WITH KEY TASKS

It is a good idea to use your diary to remind you of key tasks and key dates, and you can also pencil in time for doing A1 activities. Find out when your 'internal prime time'[3] is, the time of day when you know that you find it easy to concentrate and can work well. For some of us this is first thing in the morning, for others late afternoon or evening; try and save this time for your A1 tasks. I work best first thing in the morning, so if I have a pressing A1 I get up as early as I can and set to.

One way of protecting your 'prime time' if you work in an office, is to let others know that you will be concentrating on a key task for that part of the day. If you are a morning person you could come into the office early to get on with the A1s, or you could stay late if that suits you better.

In more enlightened organizations, some women in senior positions may be able to do certain work at home, and maintain links with colleagues via the telephone or computer. As already mentioned, the nature of work is changing, and this pattern could become the norm. It has been estimated that by 1955 there will be four million teleworkers (people working at a distance from their employer) in Britain.[4] If this is the case, you will really need to be an effective time manager. An interesting example of the potential of such a work pattern is that of F International, established in 1962 by Stephanie Shirley. Of the 70 per cent of employees working from home, 90 per cent are women.

Another concept is that of 'external prime time'[5], the time at work when others are most readily available for decisions, inquiries and information. If, for instance, your work colleagues are around in the morning, and you need their help with an A1 task, it makes sense to overlap your A1 time with parts of the 'external prime time'. It is also suggested that we don't fill up our days too tightly; we all need 'uncommitted time'.[6] This could be spent on C-type activities, and if a crisis does arise there is some space to deal with it. And, finally, given that we never know what each day will bring, try and get absolutely essential tasks out of the way as early as possible.

Relaxation and free time

A close friend once told me that she had read an article which suggested that if you really wanted to have a creative and success-ful life, you should spend at least one day a week in bed. The rationale given was that only by stopping would we allow the more creative side of the brain to function, thus giving us more imaginative ways of solving our problems. Unfortunately the domestic pressures facing most women would not easily accommodate a leisurely Sunday in bed! Nonetheless it might prove easier, and equally productive, to create some time when you can relax and do as little active thinking as possible. This really will enable you to be much more creative about difficult issues or tasks at work. You owe it to yourself to regularly build in free time, on a daily, weekly or monthly basis. You could incorporate a daily twenty-minute relaxation or meditation session, or make time to go for a walk or swim in your lunch hour.

Coping on a daily basis

So far I have given some general suggestions for managing your time. What could you do as a matter of course each day? How about making a daily 'to do' list? You could sit down first thing every morning, or last thing at night, and jot down all the things that need to be done. You could use the ABC method to see if there are any tasks which you could pass on to others. Ask yourself who might do the job more quickly and easily, or you could suggest short cuts you might not notice? Delete any task that is not essential by looking at the C activities and asking yourself, 'What is the worst thing that could happen if I didn't get round to doing this task at all?' If the consequences are not very serious you could think about ditching the activity altogether.

When dealing with correspondence try to remember to handle each piece of paper only once; having read a letter or memo act on it in some way, even if this means putting it in the filing tray, or dropping it into the wastepaper bin (so that it can be recycled). Write any replies required on the memo or letter itself, rather than using additional paper. If the necessary action is more complicated, make sure that you do something each time you pick up the correspondence, so that some progress is made on the job/task it represents.

Awareness of the best use of time

Don't forget to keep asking yourself what the best use of your time is right now, and act on the reply. There will be times when the answer is 'Nothing, do nothing'. Experience has taught me that stopping and having a break, particularly if the task is boring, difficult or stressful, can pay dividends. For instance whilst writing this book, if the sun was shining I would give myself permission every now and then to go and sit outside. After all, we are advised not to spend more than an hour or so in front of the word-processor without taking a short break. Doing nothing is essential; it rests my eyes, relaxes my neck and shoulder muscles, and gives me time to reflect upon what I've written so far. Allow yourself to stop what you are doing regularly and assess whether you could be doing something more useful to achieve your A tasks.

Saving time

So to sum up here are some hints for saving time:[7]

* Try to enjoy what you are doing.
* Build on successes.
* Reject outdated ideas and habits.
* First thing in the morning set priorities for the day.
* Give yourself time off, and special rewards when you've achieved A tasks.
* Try to give priority to As, not Bs and Cs.
* Have confidence in your assessment of your priorities, and stick to them in spite of difficulties.
* Ask yourself 'Would anything terrible happen if I didn't do this item?' If the answer is 'no', don't do it.
* If you seem to be procrastinating, ask yourself 'What am I avoiding?', and then try to confront it head on.
* Stop non-productive activities as quickly as possible.
* Do a lot of your thinking on paper.
* Set deadlines for yourself and others.
* Delegate everything you possibly can.
* Handle each piece of paper only once.
* Write replies to most letters on the letter itself.
* Relax and do nothing as often as possible.
* Continually ask yourself: 'What is the best use of my time right now?'

HOW AM I USING MY TIME?

If you would like a better understanding of how you are using your time at work at present, try working through the following exercises. These will give you information about your use/misuse of time, and you could then consider which of the above techniques you need to focus on to improve your time management. Also included at the end of the section is the assertive technique, 'Asking for time', which along with 'Saying No', are two important time-management techniques. What should you be saying 'No' to right now to make the best use of your time? When might you need to 'Ask for time' to ensure you make the right decisions about priorities? Finally, there is some further advice about confronting any tendency to procrastinate, and some ideas around delegation.

I hope you have found these techniques and additional exercises helpful. It is important to realize, however, that stopping to reflect on how you use your time is not a one-off business. It is something we need to do on quite a regular basis in order to focus on those responsibilities, tasks and activities which we may need to let go of. Letting go of things is never easy, particularly if we enjoy them. If, however, you want to manage your time efficiently, you need to review your priorities constantly, let go of what is no longer necessary, and keep focused on the A tasks. Not managing your time can be very stressful, and we shall now go on to explore how to manage stress more effectively. Better stress management depends on our being able to assert ourselves, and being more capable time managers.

Time Management Questionnaire 1

List the main activities with which you are involved in a 'typical' week. Try to identify the approximate amount of time you spend on each item, and rate each for its priority in terms of your organizational role.

Activities in a typical week	Time spent	Priority

Time Management Questionnaire 2

Review Time Management Questionnaire 1, and identify those activities which require either more or less time.

Activities requiring more time	Activities requiring less time

Time Management Questionnaire 3

Review Time Management Questionnaires 1 and 2 and answer the following questions.

1. Have I 'wasted time'? How much? How?

2. How much time was given to what I think is important?

3. How much time did I allocate to my priorities?

4. How organized was I each day in knowing what I wanted to achieve?

5. Did anything not 'get done' that I wished had been done, because I 'put it off' until another time?

6. Did I waste other people's time?

7. Did I set myself deadlines and meet them?

8. Did I ask myself, frequently, 'What is the best use of my time right now?'

9. Am I in control of my time, or do others control me? Is my time constantly being wasted by interruptions? Why do I allow this?

10. Is my time planned or unplanned? How much of my time can I really take to plan?

11. Are there activities that I'm taking too much time to accomplish?

12. Are there activities I shouldn't be doing at all?

13. Are there blank spaces in my workday when nothing seems to have been accomplished?

14. Could I change the usual sequence of some activities and thus manage that time better?

15. Which of the activities could be delegated to a subordinate, peer, or the boss? Why haven't I done this in the past? What will stop me now?

How to Create More Time

* List your goals and set your priorities.

* Make a 'To do' list.

* Categorize the list into: A (top priority items); B (important items); C (items that can wait until you have more time).

* Go to the Bs and assign them either to the As or the Cs.

* Start with the As, leaving the Cs for later.

* Keep asking yourself, 'What is the best use of my time right now?'

* Don't procrastinate; do it now.

Ideas for Managing Time at Work More Effectively

1. Prioritize your daily work.

2. Prepare for and group outgoing calls.

3. Set aside time for creative thinking.

4. Listen carefully and check your understanding.

5. Remain brief on the telephone.

6. Prepare for meetings.

7. Allow time for the unexpected.

8. Tackle one task at a time.

9. Get clear instructions, and give clear instructions.

10. Don't procrastinate.

11. Wherever possible handle each piece of paper only once.

12. Learn to say, 'No'.

Asking for Time

This is a very important technique for helping us assess our priorities when we are being asked to take on difficult or additional tasks.

It applies when people make requests or give orders and we are not sure of the implications of complying with what is being asked.

Asking for time is essentially that; you ask for time to think over what you are being asked. You give yourself the amount of time *you need* to consider the pros and cons of the request or order and you make the decision that is best for you. You do this in the light of your priorities and in the knowledge of the consequences of either refusing or accepting.

Here is what you do:

1. You listen carefully to the request/order/favour.

2. You clarify and make sure you understand what is being asked of you.

3. You pause, take a breath and think about what is being asked of you.

4. You acknowledge that you have understood what has been said and the feelings of the other person.

5. You say, 'I can't decide now, I need time to think about what is being asked for.'

6. Specify the amount of time you need and how and when you will notify the person about your decision, for example, by phone, by visit, by letter: in five minutes, one hour, tomorrow, next week, and so on.

Asking for time is about taking yourself seriously and valuing your time. You may need to remind yourself of your right to say, 'No' as there is no point in giving yourself the space to reflect on your priorities if you are still unable to say, 'No'!

Delegation, Elimination and Reduction of Work Tasks

1. Can the activity be delegated?

    A. Who can do the job instead of you?

    Experience has shown that the average employee is usually capable of much more than an average job.

    B. Who can do the job better than you?

    Delegate to more than one person.

    C. Who can do the job at less expense than you?

    D. By delegating can you contribute to the training and development of that person?

    E. What supplier can do the job for you as part of their service?

2. Can the activity be eliminated completely?

    Is the activity really important to the completion of your work?

3. Can the time you spend doing this activity be reduced?

    Look at each activity and see how many minutes/hours you can realistically eliminate from each. If you can't you may be too involved personally and should get someone else to analyse it for you.

Suggestions for Defeating Procrastination

1. Get started immediately on something you have been postponing. Simply beginning will help you to eliminate anxiety about the whole project.

2. When you postpone taking important actions, fear of embarrassment, rejection or failure are often at the root of the problem.
   A. Analyse your fears. Ask yourself:
       (i)   What am I afraid of?
       (ii) Is this fear real or exaggerated?
       (iii) What else can I do to increase my chances of success?

3. Set aside a designated time slot which you will devote exclusively to the task you've been putting off. Often you find that the 15 minutes of serious effort can get you over the hump of procrastination.

4. Do it now!

5. Use the 'Swiss cheese' technique. When procrastinating on a major task, break it up into as many small manageable 'instant tasks' as possible. This way you make holes in the project.

6. Be courageous about undertaking an activity that you've been avoiding. One act of courage can eliminate all that fear. Stop telling yourself you must perform well. Remind yourself that doing it is far more important.

ATS – Stress Management

Stress management is the third and final part of the model we have been exploring. As always, the central issue is our right to speak out about our experiences at work, including stress. It has rarely felt safe to talk about how stressed we may be feeling in the male world of work. It may be very hard to cope assertively with stress for fear that we will be judged as lacking, or personally inadequate, in some way. However, we need to assert ourselves if we are to manage our stress, and we need to know how to protect our time assertively if we are to function well at work.

UNDERSTANDING STRESS

In this section you will find definitions of stress, personal accounts of how stress has affected women at work and a number of practical ways of coping with it. For many of us work is becoming increasingly stressful. This is due in part to the cycles of recession and growth in the world economy, and decisions being made at both national and local levels to reduce public spending within local government, the Health Service and numerous voluntary sector organizations. Private sector businesses and firms are suffering too, and the early 1990s have seen wide-scale redundancies. These changes create more pressure on employees and, as women new to this world, we may worry that we will be the first to go when times get hard. This uncertainty about the future creates stress.

What can we do about stress? Working women need to let themselves talk about their stress; by sharing the problem with others the common themes emerge and we can start to identify better ways of coping. Many of us react to stress by over-eating, smoking or drinking too much, or losing our tempers. These actions may help in the short term, but actually create more problems in the long run. For instance, whilst men are giving up smoking, more women, and in particular young women, are taking it up. The number of women attending centres for alcohol and drug abuse has risen dramatically in the last decade, and many women have a recurrent weight problem which, in extreme cases, can strain the heart and lead to a wide range of health problems. We must ascertain what creates stress for us, and find a range of solutions for coping better. Being more assertive, and managing our time more effectively, can both help, but firstly we need to understand the causes of stress at work.

Although stress affects women at all levels, women managers have been identified as a group experiencing considerable stress. However, the relevant issues are the same for all working women: women experience stress, but because the rules of the game are male defined, and rarely mirror the values, behaviours and skills they bring to the workplace, many women find themselves being devalued for their lack of aggression/drive rather than respected for their superior relationship-building and communication skills.

Women are skilful and talented and bring enormous creativity and humanity into the workplace. This is particularly true of women who have brought up a family, and have had to develop a whole range of skills in managing the home. Work, however, still reflects the values of the wider society, and thus women's ability to display co-operation rather than competition, concern for others, and superior listening, communication and interpersonal skills, are not generally noticed or appreciated. In fact, many women are deemed weak because they fail to show the aggressive, selfish behaviour which ear-marked the organizational style of the 1980s. Work can be highly competitive because male socialization reinforces aggressive competitive behaviour. This means the workplace is stressful for both genders, but perhaps women are still considerably disadvantaged because of some specific stresses:[1]

* Being the token woman.
* Lack of same-sex role models.
* Performance pressures.
* Sex a disadvantage re job promotion/career prospects.
* Sex discrimination and prejudice generally.

* Colleagues of opposite sex treated more favourably by senior management.
* Sexual harassment.
* Lack of encouragement from senior staff.
* Lack of social support from people at work.
* Being single and labelled as an 'oddity'.
* Career-related dilemma concerning whether to start a family; whether to marry/live with someone.

Do any of the above apply to you? If so, what are the consequences in terms of your ability to feel comfortable at work?

STRESSFUL SITUATIONS

Outlined below are some examples of difficult situations that women have found themselves in at work, which made life very uncomfortable and potentially very stressful. Does any of this remind you of your own experiences?

College Lecturer

I work in a mainly female environment; at the moment all my close colleagues, except for my Head of Department, are women. Though he only works part-time on the course, he sets the standards and ethos and most decisions are referred to him – he really dominates what is going on even when he's not there. He is aware of this, or at least has been told this, and I think has tried to make some effort to let go, but can't. We have been likened to spinning tops; every now and then he cracks the whip and we all spin as he wants us to. The problem is made more difficult because he is having an affair with the course tutor. Neither of them have ever told me this, but other staff know. Their behaviour is impeccable on the surface, and none of the students have guessed. But it means that the course tutor will not challenge him, and her authority is undermined. The other full-time member of staff does challenge him, and this often creates an 'atmosphere'. I feel on the edge of this, and not sure what I should do for the best. I know I feel some of my autonomy as a teacher is being taken away.

Catering Manager

I once worked in a clothing factory, where the machinists were all women but the managers were men. I really felt put in my place.

The women were to cook, sew and be sex objects, but that was all. My post was Catering Manager; I never called myself manageress, as I felt this compromised my sex, and I never felt I was given the status the job involved. The manager of the firm, who had employed me, was rather lecherous. I left the job after six months as I didn't feel respected as a professional, and wasn't prepared to put up with the sexist behaviour of the boss any longer.

Drama Teacher

This year my boss retired, and I applied for his post. I have specialist qualifications in the field, considerable and varied experience, and have proved over the past eighteen months (during my boss's prolonged illness) that I am capable of organizing and running the department. I was not even granted an interview; in fact no women were shortlisted. I did, however, have the opportunity of speaking to higher management about this. I was already hurt and somewhat puzzled over why I had been overlooked. The interview was a pat on the head; I was told what a good girl (at forty-four years of age!) I was, and how hard I had worked, and how they valued my contribution. But didn't I think I was flying too high, too soon – I wasn't really ready for the job, was I? I am of small physique possibly quite feminine, and really wonder if they would have spoken to any of my male colleagues in this way.

Probation Officer

I remember feeling quite vulnerable. I just have this image in my mind of years and years working in a court setting, in a sea of court officers and jailers, and being very conscious of the kind of asides that would go on between them; you know, personal comments about me. I know that I actually allowed this to happen and played along with it because I knew I needed a good working relationship with the male police officers and jailers in order to do my job. Unfortunately, this relationship was based on allowing them to behave in a sexist, flirtatious kind of way with me. . .

These are just a few examples of what many women have to put up with on a day-to-day basis in their workplaces. Many of them experience stress as a result. Some of this stress could have been relieved or even prevented if they had been able to assert themselves and stand up for their rights in certain situations. The right, for example, to stand up for professional autonomy; to challenge sexist behaviour which borders on sexual harassment; to challenge false assumptions about competence as a woman; and finally to refuse to collude with a sexist culture. None of these things are easy, but until we demand better treatment nothing is going to change.

WOMEN RETURNERS

We are now in a much more powerful position to make demands on employers, for they want our skills and labour. They are prepared to go to greater efforts to get us back into the workplace, and keep us there. The carrots being used are work-based crèches, flexi-time and job-share arrangements, and a willingness to help us manage our career breaks. It is only now dawning on employers, faced with a diminishing adolescent workforce, that the skills women have developed in the domestic sphere are relevant to the needs of industry. This places women returners in a particularly strong position, and we need to capitalize on this.

Unfortunately, a woman returning to the workplace has to suffer for a short period of time, the oppressive notion of 'Superwoman'. Women at work, and women with the dual roles of employment and family responsibilities, have been thought capable of doing it all, and still look like Shirley Conran (and write best-selling novels!). Fortunately, the notion of Superwoman is taking a firm nose-dive, but many women are still under enormous pressure to do it all *and* get it right. For instance, most working women still have the major responsibility for managing the domestic sphere in addition to a full- or part-time job.

In particular, women are still held to be responsible for:

* Dependents at home.
* Providing emotional support for partners, children and extended family and friends.
* Ensuring that domestic chores get done.
* Ensuring that food is bought, and prepared.
* Catering for family friends and visitors.

Many women are expected to manage all this without the kind of domestic support they are giving their partners, or their male colleagues are receiving at home. The fact that many of us seem to cope with this situation does not mean it is without cost, and many of us may be suffering from the symptoms of stress, such as tiredness, tension headaches, increased smoking, drinking, eating, or misuse of prescribed drugs. Whilst enabling us to cope in the short-term, these may be damaging our health and well-being in the long-term. Unfortunately, as many women feel guilty about asserting their needs for space, relaxation and nurturing, they may muddle along like this for years. They may wait for ever – for the children to become fully independent, their husbands to satisfy their career aspirations, and their parents to cope with the ageing process – for the time when it is okay to get *their* needs met.

If we have never considered we have the right to look after ourselves and our physical well-being, we may not recognize the signs of stress; indeed, many of us accept stress symptoms as normal. Recognizing stress demands time to stop and look at what you are doing in your life, at what cost to yourself, and what options you have to do things differently.

WHAT IS STRESS?

A useful definition of stress taken from NEC, *Stress Management*. 1989, is as follows:

High Demands plus High Constraints, plus Low Support = Stress

This definition allows us to view stress as both an individual and organizational issue.

Stress from an individual perspective

* Working women can make very high demands on themselves by having very high expectations of what they should achieve, that is being the perfect mother, and best secretary/boss.

* Working women can be operating under enormous constraints or pressure, that is, having to cope with two jobs, one of which is in paid employment.

* If they are unable or unwilling to get support from friends, family or their organization, the end result is likely to be one of experiencing stress; many women think they have to get on and cope with everything by themselves.

Stress from the organizational perspective

* If an organization places high demands on a female employee.
* If it is unable or unwilling to provide the resources to enable the woman to meet these demands, because of limited time, money or staffing levels.
* If no support is provided for the female employee in this situation the outcome is again likely to be one of stress.

Test your stress level

One way of seeing whether you may be experiencing stress or not is to read through and answer the following questionnaire. It may indicate your major sources of stress at work.

Having identified that you may be experiencing stress, it may help to have some clarity about the physical, emotional and behavioural signs of stress:

Physical signs
* palpitations — throbbing heart
* pain and tightness in the chest
* indigestion
* breathlessness
* nausea
* muscle twitches
* tiredness
* headaches
* vague aches or pains
* skin irritation or rashes
* susceptibility to allergies
* clenched fists or jaw
* fainting
* frequent colds, 'flu or other infections
* recurrence of previous illnesses
* constipation or diarrhoea
* rapid weight gain or loss
* alteration of the menstrual pattern in women

Emotional signs

* swings in mood
* increased worrying

Stress Questionnaire

What causes you stress at work?

Workload   Yes   No
1. Do you have about the right amount of work to do?
2. Can you complete your work in the time available?
3. Can you meet deadlines?
4. Can you take short breaks at work?
5. Do you have enough variety in your work?

Feelings at work
1. Do you feel that your work is worthwhile?
2. Do you feel involved in your work?
3. Do you feel that others value and appreciate your work?
4. Can you do your work the way you want to?

Workplace
1. Do you have sufficient space to work in?
2. Is your workplace quiet enough?
3. Is your workplace well cared for?
4. Is your workplace conducive to the sort of work you have to do in it?
5. Do you have sufficient privacy in your workplace?
6. Do you have a place you can call your own at work?

Colleagues
1. Do you enjoy working with most of your colleagues?
2. Can you discuss work problems with them?
3. Do they help and support you when you need it?
4. Are your colleagues sensitive to issues of sexism and racism?

Supervisor/Boss
1. Does your supervisor/boss help you when you need it?
2. Does he/she give you clear feedback about the quality of your work?
3. Does he/she praise you when you've done something well?
4. Does he/she give you constructive criticism about your work?
5. Does he/she help you to do your job better?

Role within your organization
1. Are you clear about what is expected of you at work?
2. Do you have a job description?
3. Do the people with whom you come into contact understand your job and accept the way you do it?
4. Do you have the opportunity to develop and improve your skills?
5. Do you have the right amount of responsibility for your skills?
6. Is your job secure?
7. Are you kept well informed about any changes in your job?
8. Do you have the resources to do your job properly?
9. Are you paid fairly for the job?

(Source: *Stress Management*, NEC, 1989.)

* irritability
* feeling tense
* drained, no enthusiasm
* cynical
* feeling nervous, apprehensive, anxious
* feelings of helplessness
* loss of confidence
* lack of self-esteem
* lack of concentration
* withdrawal into day-dreams

Behavioural signs

* accident proneness
* poor work
* increased smoking
* increased dependence on drugs
* overeating or loss of appetite
* change in sleep pattern, difficulty in getting to sleep and waking tired
* loss of interest in sex
* poor time management
* impaired speech
* withdrawal from supportive relationships
* taking work home more
* too busy to relax
* not looking after oneself

The following list of symptoms need to be taken seriously:

* recurrent headaches
* ringing in the ears or frequent head noises
* frequent use of self-prescribed drugs
* palpitation and chest pain
* frequent heartburn, stomach cramps, diarrhoea, being full of gas, unable to swallow
* feeling that you may pass out
* getting any illness that is around
* loss of former concentration
* loss of former reliable memory
* a new difficulty in thinking around problems
* a new inability to reach satisfactory decisions
* a feeling of being very low or dulled

* a shut-down in all emotions except anger and irritation
* all joy, laughter and pleasure have dried up
* active love and caring have lessened or disappeared
* tears seem frequently very near for no reason

(Source: *Understanding Stress*, HMSO, 1987).

Assessing your stress

Having read through this, do you think you are suffering from stress and, if so, how much? Do you understand the causes of any stress you are suffering? This may be as a result of your personal life and the responsibilities you have there. Is there anything that you could change to decrease the amount of stress you are experiencing in that area? Could you manage your time better by letting go of some of the tasks you set yourself at home? Do you need to have such high standards, or could you get others, such as members of the family or paid help to help you with the housework?

Are you taking on too much responsiblity for the problems of others at home? Do you need to think about your right to 'decline responsibility for others' problems'? Could you be exercising your right to say 'No' more often? Think about how much you expect of yourself, and how realistic this is in view of your responsibilities at work. Ask yourself how much others may take you for granted, and see if there are things that you could delegate. Do you still need to do things for your children or partner? Couldn't they start doing these things for themselves?

As you review your home life you may see many ways of reducing stress by managing your time and asserting yourself more effectively. It might help quickly to review the Bill of Rights (see pages 19–20) and talk with other women about the techniques they have employed to stand up for themselves at home and with their immediate and extended families.

CAUSES OF STRESS IN THE WORKPLACE

We must now focus attention on the causes of stress in the workplace. Read slowly through the following list and see which points apply to you.

Physical environment

You will probably experience stress at work if you have poor physical conditions which include:

* insufficient space
* lack of privacy
* open plan
* inhuman layout
* too hot or too cold
* badly lit
* too noisy
* poor ventilation

The organization

You will experience stress at work if the organization has:

* insufficient staff for the size of the workload
* too many unfilled posts
* poor co-ordination between departments
* insufficient training to do the job well
* inadequate information given
* no control over workload
* rigid working procedures
* no time given to adjust to changes

The way the organization is managed

You may experience stress at work if the organization is managed in such a way that there is:

* inconsistency in style and approach of your managers
* emphasis on competitiveness
* crisis management all the time
* information seen as power and thus withheld from you
* procedures always being changed
* over-dependence on overtime
* shift work

Role in the organization

You may experience stress at work if in your job:

* your work role is ambiguously defined
* you have major conflicts of interest in your role
* too little responsibility
* no participation in decision-making
* lack of managerial support
* responsibility for people and things

Relating with the organization

You may experience stress at work if your relationships in the organization include:

* poor relations with the boss
* poor relations with colleagues and subordinates
* difficulties in delegating responsibility
* personality conflicts
* no feedback from colleagues or management

Career development

You may experience stress at work if your career development is characterized by:

* lack of job security
* over-promotion
* under-promotion
* thwarted ambition
* job has insufficient status
* not paid as well as others who do similar jobs

Personal and social relationships

You may experience stress at work if your personal and social relationships are characterized by:

* not enough opportunities for social contact while at work
* sexism and sexual harassment
* racism and racial harassment
* conflicts with family demands
* divided loyalties between your own needs and organizational demands

Equipment

You may experience stress at work if the equipment you use is:
* not suitable for the job or environment
* old and/or in poor condition
* unreliable/or not maintained regularly/constant breakdowns
* badly sited
* requires individual to adopt fixed and uncomfortable posture
* adds to noise and heat levels

Stress at home

You may experience stress at work if you are also having to cope with any of the following stresses at home:
* death of a family member
* marriage, separation or divorce
* birth of a child
* problems with parents
* health problems of a family member
* partner is made redundant
* you move house
* your child leaves home

COPING WITH STRESS

If you are suffering from any of these stresses it is likely that this will affect your performance at work. Talk to your colleagues about it and get their support. If you think you will get a sympathetic hearing it might be useful to approach your manager and let her/him know the situation. Some workplaces now employ specially trained staff to help with stress-related problems. You might also consider approaching a union representative to see what is available through the union.

Care, support and time

It is important to be gentle with yourself, and appreciate how stressful any changes in lifestyle and working situation are. We often assume we should just get on and cope with changes in our lives, such as the loss of a parent or the birth of a child. These are difficult times, and you owe it to yourself to get the necessary help and support. In previous generations the extended family network offered us guidance and support; with the current trend to greater geographical mobility we may only have ourselves and our friends to rely on. Allow yourself to admit to the time, care and help you need to cope with painful and difficult transitions.

Medical check-up

If you have identified yourself as someone suffering from stress it would be as well to have a full medical check-up. Your GP may be willing to do this, but it is more likely you will have to pay a private practitioner. Talk to friends, consult Yellow Pages, and phone up to check out prices. Remember you need to take stress seriously, as the following diseases have been linked to it to varying degrees.

Coronary Heart Disease This is the biggest killer in the Western world. Studies have revealed a positive link between competitive, aggressive behaviour and coronary heart disease. Think about what we were saying earlier about the nature of work, and the emphasis on aggression.

Cancer There has been considerable research into the relationship between stress and cancer, and it appears that people prone to symptoms of stress, such as anger, fear and feelings of helplessness, are more susceptible to cancer. How fearful do you feel at work? How often do you feel helpless to really create the type of work environment you want to be involved in?

Digestive disorders Persistent indigestion is indicative that we are experiencing stress. It is estimated that one person in ten will get an ulcer at some time, and every year millions of working days are lost because of them.

Diabetes Diabetes often follows a physical or emotional upset to the system. Adult onset of diabetes is becoming increasingly common in this country.

We need to become aware of how our bodies are responding to the stress we are experiencing. We must learn to respect this information, and take positive action, rather than ignoring the evidence and trying to push ourselves even harder.

Alternative therapies

We could try an alternative practitioner. Many GPs are becoming aware that a more holistic approach can be of benefit to their patients, but unfortunately do not always have the time or the resources to respond in this manner themselves. So, although it is a good idea to see your GP first, think about approaching a holistic practitioner too. Choose a reputable name by contacting the Council for Complementary and Alternative Medicine (the address is in the Resources section at the end of the book).

Some popular types of holistic medicine are as follows:

Osteopathy

This is a physical therapy used to restore and maintain the skeletal, muscular, nervous and circulatory systems of the body. Imbalance is thought to be caused by physical strain or injury, psychological stress or general lifestyle, resulting in neck and back pain, digestive upsets, menstrual disorders and respiratory problems. The osteopath's role is to seek and treat the cause of the disease and, by gentle techniques, restore normal functioning.

Acupuncture

A therapy that is used to restore and maintain health as well as to prevent illness. When the body or mind produces physical or mental symptoms, there is an imbalance of vital energy in the body (known as *Ch'i* in Chinese medicine). By inserting fine needles the acupuncturist can direct and rebalance this energy, thus improving the general level of health as well as dealing with the underlying cause of the symptoms.

Homoeopathy

A system of medicine which uses the natural 'law of similars', meaning that something which causes symptoms can also cure it, to stimulate and assist the body's ability to cure itself. Ill health is viewed by the homoeopath as an expression of disorder within the whole person, which the body is attempting to heal by itself. The homoeopath helps this process by directly stimulating the individual's vitality.

Massage therapy

Massage is one of the oldest forms of therapy. Holistic massage works on two levels: physically, it can relieve back pain and headaches, and at an emotional level a good massage can soothe stress and tension, create feelings of well-being and enhance self-esteem.

Alexander technique

This technique is a preventive as well as a therapeutic treatment. It changes individual habits of thought, feelings and movement. The Alexander teacher helps the individual learn how to use the right amount of effort in everyday activities, such as sitting, standing and walking, which results in a reduction of the stress previously caused by the body's imbalance.

Shiatsu

According to Shiatsu, physical and emotional discomforts are an imbalance of energy, expressed via backache, headaches, mental depression, and so on. The Shiatsu practitioner applies pressure to energy channels in the body, stimulating areas of need and dispersing from areas of congestion, thus restoring balance to the whole body.

Increase your awareness

Become knowledgeable about stress

* Identify your major sources of stress.
* Anticipate stressful periods and plan for them.
* Develop a number of constructive strategies and practise them.

Come to terms with your feelings

* Do not suppress your feelings: acknowledge them to yourself and share them with others.
* Learn to be flexible and adaptable.

Develop effective behavioural skills

* Do not use the words 'can not' when you actually mean 'will not'.
* Use free time productively.
* Be assertive.

* Avoid blaming others for situations.
* Provide positive feedback to others.
* Learn to say 'No'.
* Acknowledge problems as soon as they appear.

Establish and maintain a strong support network

* Ask for direct help, and be receptive to it when it is offered.
* Rid yourself of dead or damaging relationships.
* Tell the members of your support network that you value the relationship.

Develop a lifestyle that will strengthen you against stress

* Maintain correct weight.
* Regularly practise some form of exercise: vigorous, stretching, recreational.
* Engage regularly in some form of systematic relaxation.
* Use alcohol and caffeine in moderation, or not at all.
* Do not use tobacco.
* Avoid foods high in sugar, salt, white flour, saturated fats, chemicals.
* Plan your use of time, both daily and on a long-term basis.
* Seek out variety and change of pace.
* Do not dwell on unimportant matters.

Remember your spiritual development

* Establish a sense of purpose and direction.
* Believe in yourself.
* Learn to transcend stressful situations: maintain a sense of proportion.

(Source: *Stress Management*, NEC, 1989.)

Meditation

Meditation is one of the most helpful psychological techniques available to us in countering stress. Frequent and regular meditation:

* trains the attention
* increases control over thought processes

* increases the ability to handle emotions
* aids physical relaxation

Awareness/meditation exercise

This is an exercise you can do on your own to help practice meditation. It might help to tape the instructions so that you can listen to them as you relax. Alternatively, ask a friend to read them out for you, in a slow, clear voice.

Sit comfortably, both feet on the floor, back alert but supported. Close eyes.

Follow your breath . . . just following it as it enters and leaves the body . . . not trying to change it . . . just allowing it to be as it is . . .

Become aware of any sounds around you.

Become aware of your body . . . of any sensations . . . any aches or pains . . . any tension . . . just allowing it to be there, not trying to change it . . .

Become aware of any feelings and emotions . . . noticing them without labelling them or trying to change them, feeling them just as they are . . .

Become aware of any internal commentary or thoughts, allowing them to flow through . . . like watching a film . . . not holding on, just letting them go.

Bring your attention to your body and as you do this, see whether there is a word or a phrase or image which describes just how it is to be you right now . . .

Stay for a moment with the word, phrase or image . . . checking out whether it does fit . . .

Then let it go . . . as you come back to the breath . . . rising and falling . . . just allowing it to be as it is . . .

Repeat the process, all the while being aware of the breath, for ten to twenty minutes. When you are ready, open your eyes and focus your attention on the things around you.

(Adapted from *Focusing* by Eugene Gendlin.)

Guidelines for meditation

1. Choose a quiet spot where you will not be disturbed by other people or the telephone.
2. Sit in a comfortable position with your back straight and legs uncrossed (unless you choose to sit crosslegged on a floor cushion).

3. Relax your muscles sequentially from head to feet, being aware of each part of your body in succession, and letting go of the tension in each area with a sigh of relief.
4. Meditate with your eyes closed. If you become drowsy you can open them for a while and look around you.
5. Become aware of your breathing, noticing how it passes in and out, without trying to control it in any way. As soon as you notice your mind has wandered, simply bring your attention back to your breath.
6. If you become anxious, angry (unexpressed or suppressed emotions are sometimes released as you meditate) or you start judging how you are doing, simply label what you notice your mind is doing and return your awareness back to your breath.
7. Practise at least once a day for ten to twenty minutes. Don't do too much in the early days, as you may find it too difficult.

Relaxation technique

Choose a quiet room and a time when you're unlikely to be disturbed.
Wear light clothing.
Lie on your back on the floor or a firm surface.
Tense the muscles in your right foot and ankle. Clench the muscles and release them several times.
Repeat the exercise with your left foot and ankle.
Tense the calf muscles, first one then the other. Repeat several times alternatively, clenching and unclenching.
Move next to the thigh muscles, and carry out the same exercise.
Next move to the muscles of the buttocks.
Work upwards, tensing in turn the muscles of the abdomen, chest, back and shoulders.
Next move to the biceps, forearms and hands.
Lastly the neck, the jaw, the face and the forehead and scalp.

Diet

People experiencing stress may have a tendency to under- or over-eat, or to eat rushed, insubstantial meals.[2] As the body uses up more energy than usual under stress a healthy diet is really important. At the same time additional strain is placed on the heart, and so it is sensible to follow what has been called a 'heart-saver diet'. The main principles behind this diet are as follows:

* Cut down the intake of fat. Adults should eat no more than 80g of fat per day.
* Eat as much fresh fruit and vegetables as possible, raw if you can. Steam rather than boil vegetables.
* Eat as much fibre as possible, in the form of wholemeal bread, fibre-rich breakfast cereals, the skins of fruits and vegetables.
* Cut down on sugar and salt. Use them only sparingly in cooking and never add them to food at the table.
* Cook your own food rather than eating out or buying convenience food.
* Take a good Vitamin B supplement containing all the vitamins in the B range.
* Watch your weight – we should actually lose a little weight from middle age onwards if we're to stay fit.

Letting go of emotions

There is general agreement[3] that consistent repression of the emotions can lead to psychological problems. This is particularly true if this is a blanket repression, with all emotions constantly repressed, rather than a selective kind, where certain emotions are repressed in certain circumstances. The psychological problems created by blanket repression include inner conflicts, depression, obsessionality, self-rejection and vague, free-floating anxiety.

Because of what we know already about the relationship between stress and disease, it is essential that we allow ourselves to experience all our emotions. David Fontana suggests that we should find safe places to express our emotions.[4] If it doesn't feel safe at work, or at home, then go somewhere where you can be on your own or with people you trust, and let out your emotions by screaming and shouting, stamping you feet in rage or crying in despair. Similarly we may also need to hop and skip for joy, or laugh hysterically at some amusing situation.

Whatever your need for emotional expression, it's important not to forget how important crying is in coping with stress. Crying alters the body's chemistry, reversing some of the harmful physiological stress reactions. It has been suggested that the lower incidence of early heart disease in women is linked in part of their ability to break down and weep when they feel the need. Owing to the prejudice of others, it may be inappropriate for you to cry in public, but find the time and place to shed those tears. You have a right to look after your psychological well-being by crying when you feel safe to do so.

Exercise

Physical exercise has an important part to play in reducing the effects of stress. Physical exercise helps discharge tense, stored-up energy, and helps the mind focus on things other than the pressures and frustrations of work. People who take regular physical exercise tend to have more energy, feel better in themselves, and are less susceptible to stress-related diseases, in particular heart attacks and strokes.

As young women we may well have been encouraged to exercise and taken part in sports, but as we get older many of us don't make the time for regular exercise. Perhaps it is related to those notions of femininity that 'nice' girls don't sweat, but look neat and tidy all the time. We may also feel that we don't have the right to take time out for ourselves; it would be selfish to spend time at the sports centre when we should be doing some essential tasks at home for the family. Post Jane Fonda attitudes have changed, and many younger women now exercise regularly. Sadly the private leisure industry has become very exclusive and expensive, and enormous pressure is placed on young people to have the right sports clothes. However, there is a range of sport facilities available for everyone, regardless of income, so long as you are prepared to acknowledge your right for space to take care of your physical and mental well-being, and can manage your time more effectively to create that space.

It's important to find the sport or exercise that you really want to do, rather than one that you think is good for you. Many people enjoy walking, but rarely do much on a daily basis. Perhaps you could walk to work, or to the shops occasionally, if this is within a reasonable distance. Maybe you could use public transport more often; this would not only help your physical health, but that of the planet as well. A Sunday afternoon stroll may suit the whole family; or a family visit to a leisure pool or sports centre could greatly benefit our level of fitness. Outings of this sort are not cheap; we have to reorganize our priorities and put additional resources, such as time and money, aside to achieve more balance in our lives.

The range of activities available includes walking, swimming, dancing, fitness classes, aerobics, ball games (including tennis and squash), working out in a gym and a host of others. Some can be done on your own, perhaps in the lunch time; others may be more fun if done with a friend or in a group. Going out on a Sunday for a long walk with a group of friends can be great fun so long as you dress appropriately, and choose a suitable route and distance. Belonging to a sports club can give you an additional string to your social life, and get you fit at the same time. If you really wanted to treat yourself, you might think about visiting a health farm for the day, or a long weekend. This could give you the necessary boost to start to build in time for exercise on a regular basis.

Here are some guidelines for starting the process of getting fit:

1. Initially, exercise every day. Once you have reached a desired level of fitness, reduce to three times a week and you can still maintain this level.
2. Each exercise session should last a minimum of 20 minutes. Shorter periods don't allow the body to produce the desired changes that constitute fitness.

Remember the adage – *Use it or lose it!* You have the right to be fit, and it will help you in managing work-related stress. If, however, you think you may be very out of condition, or are over the age of thirty-five, check with your GP before starting any intensive exercise programme. Don't push yourself too hard to start with, in your enthusiasm to get fitter. You don't have to give yourself a hard time to become fit, and it could be dangerous. If your initial enthusiasm wears off, and you don't enjoy the exercise of your choice find something that suits you and you'll be able to keep going with it.

Communicating our problems to others

We need to communicate our problems to others when we are going through a difficult time. This may mean talking things over with our partner, if we have one, or a close friend. At other times it may mean seeking out the help of a counsellor, consultant or therapist. It is important to let ourselves get the support we need, but also to respect that others cannot always give us everything we require. You can place great strain on your relationships if you over-use the support on offer, and it is important that you seek help from a number of sources rather than relying on one or two people who are close to you, who may need to retreat from you in order not to feel overwhelmed. At such times, seeking the help of a counsellor or therapist would be of great benefit.

We all need to have a support network, and it would be useful now to go through the list below thinking of the people who provide the various types of support for you. If you find that the same name keeps coming up this may indicate that you are too dependent upon that individual, and need to spread the load around a bit more. If this person was to disappear from your life, how would you get the support you needed? Think about who could give you this support, and how you might develop the relationship in order to get what you want. You, of course, will need to be offering something in return, but this clarity will help you enormously in developing your network.

Support network

* Someone I can rely on in a crisis.
* Someone who makes me feel good about myself.
* Someone I can be totally myself with.
* Someone who will tell me how well or badly I am doing.
* Someone I can talk to if worried.
* Someone who really makes me stop and think about what I am doing.
* Someone who is lively to be with.
* Someone who introduces me to new ideas, new interests, new people.

(Source: *Stress Management*, NEC, 1989.)

Reappraising your life

It's very easy for us to become so overwhelmed by stress that we don't take the time to stand back and reappraise what we are doing and where we are going, which is vital to our well-being. As women working in organizations, we need to think about:

* Are we in the right job?
* Is it taking us in the right direction?
* Have we the right skills to make a success of the job?
* Are we relating well to others?
* What are our long- and short-term priorities?
* What is good about our lives, and what do we need to change?

In the rush of daily life it is important not to forget that this is it; this is not a rehearsal, and we need to be clear that we are getting what we want from this life. Start to give yourself permission to have time for yourself, to live in the moment and enjoy the life you have now, rather than waiting for that magic time in the future when things will be exactly as you want.

We shall be exploring these themes in more detail in the chapter on life and career planning, but once again we can see the relationship with assertion. It is really important to be clear in life: clear about what we want as women, and able to communicate this to the people in our lives. We may then have to cope with their feelings of anger, disappointment or disapproval, but honest interaction is much better for all involved in the long run. It will actually stop a lot of heartache, disease and stress if you can speak out and own up to your thoughts and feelings, rather than non-assertively going along with others' expectations and assumptions about what you need.

Before we move on, read through the following list and see which of these things apply to you. Write out your own list and place it somewhere central so you can be reminded of your options at times of stress.

Checklist for coping with stress

* become knowledgeable about stress
* recognize your personal limits
* reduce stress levels by planning and prioritizing
* develop a lifestyle that will act as a buffer against the effects of stress
* keep physically fit
* follow a balanced diet
* take regular exercise
* avoid all drugs
* create leisure time
* get adequate rest and sleep
* practise breathing control
* deliberately relax
* manage your time
* have clear objectives
* be more assertive
* be clear about your values
* challenge unreasonable demands and deadlines

* develop an effective support system
* share problems with others

Learning to cope with stressful situations

Finally, spend some time thinking about situations which you find stressful, at home or work. Consider ways in which you could reduce this stress, perhaps by being more assertive, managing your time better, practising deep breathing or relaxation techniques. By giving yourself the chance to be clear now, you will find the situation a lot easier to handle next time.

Complete the following grid as honestly and as creatively as you can.

Stressful situation	Coping strategy

4

Life and Career Planning

If better time management is based on prioritizing, and making the best use of time on a daily basis, then life and career planning is concerned with having clarity about our long-term goals. It requires a willingness to assess who we are and what we want; reviewing our skills, beliefs and values; and taking responsibility for creating home and work situations which honour our needs and potential as human beings.

This is in marked contrast to the lack of responsibility shown by the passive, 'non-assertive' female stereotype. Women are actively encouraged to be non-assertive about their needs, with the result that they find it hard to know what they really require from life. For many women, the men in their lives have assumed the right to make decisions about the major 'life decisions'. Thus women's potential is often contained within the employment/career needs of their partners, and the decisions taken will be those that enhance men's potential and work prospects.

This may seem a rather narrow, out-dated view, given the fact that over 40 per cent of women are in paid employment, and an increasing number are climbing the organizational ladder. The majority of women, however, have jobs rather than careers. Their employment is fitted in around their partners' life plans and the needs of children and ageing relatives. Indeed, recent changes in health and social services provision, and concepts such as 'care in the community', mean that the needs of the physically and mentally ill will increasingly be met by the women in 'the community'! In view of women's inbuilt concern for the welfare of others, should we really find this a problem? After all, if we don't meet our responsibilities towards members of our family, who will? The problem is, of course, that such assumptions about women's capacity as carers is based on the premise that women don't really need to work, whereas research suggests that the vast majority do, and for financial reasons.[1]

THE IMPORTANCE OF PLANNING FOR THE FUTURE

If a woman has financial difficulties this may stem from a variety of sources, such as inadequate income of the partner, higher cost of living, and punishingly steep interest and mortgage rates. At the same time many women choose to live independently of conventional relationships, and others are forced to, owing to relationship breakdowns. One in three marriages ends in divorce, and many more women are opting to leave unsatisfactory relationships or marriages. This means ever-increasing financial burdens for women, many of whom support offspring. How, then, do women find the time and energy to support both themselves and their children, and the needs of members of their extended family, who may be ill or infirm? What options are open to women caring for their elderly parents? Could this affect you in a few years' time, and how will you manage given your present home, work situation and income level?

We need to face up to the fact that paid employment is important to women. It is foolish to assume our financial security is someone else's responsibility, and the lives of thousands of single, separated, divorced and elderly women are a testament to the folly of this particular belief system. We need to wise up and think about the implications of the life-decisions facing us; we must set goals, and make plans which keep a range of options open, so that we can cope with our future, however it turns out. If we do not face up to this we run the risk of enforced membership of the growing band of women living on inadequate incomes, either through low wages, low income support or miserably inadequate state pensions.

We can forestall the 'poverty trap' by honestly evaluating our lives and our futures now. This may mean training for employment which is more secure and better paid or, for instance, starting a savings plan, and making provision for an adequate pension. The right decisions now could protect you from money problems resulting from relationship breakups or fluctuating economic trends. It is in our interests to start taking responsibility for planning for future job satisfaction and security, greater financial rewards, and a fulfilling home and social life.

Our lack of willingness to do this in the past has been related to our feelings of low self-esteem. We probably felt grateful for the little we were receiving, and didn't want to rock the boat for fear that what we had might be taken away. This can be true for many women at work, even those at quite senior levels. According to a black woman consultant many feel vulnerable about their security in the workplace.[2] She says:

> I think that a lot of women, even at senior levels, aren't really that confident in their positions or themselves, and I suspect that many of them probably think that one day somebody is going to tap them on the shoulder, 'Ah, this is a mistake, we didn't really mean to make you to be director of this department'. They're working in this frame of mind that it's all a dream, and if I don't push myself to the Nth degree, I'm going to wake up one day and find myself back at the bottom of the heap again.

Many of us do not have job security; we are already part of the flexible labour force identified by Charles Handy in *The Age of Unreason*. We can be taken on or laid off by employers according to economic trends. There is an insufficient number of us with the skills, experience and qualifications which would make us indispensable to an organization shedding staff. In addition, there is still a tendency, in periods of economic recession, to revert to the old idea that it is men that are entitled to scarce jobs. According to Barron and Norris (1976):

> Women are commonly held to be more dispensable than men ... because of the strength of family values, and even when a woman's income may be vital to family living standards, it is often said that her real place is in the home with her family and that her husband is or should be the main source of income.

How many of us would be qualified to join the 'core workers' of professionals, technicians and managers of the future? On reflection, many of us would not choose to make the extreme personal, physical and mental sacrifices which membership of the 'core' demands. We do, however, need to take our time and worth more seriously if we are to secure a safer future. At present, women rarely earn an income commensurate with the amount of effort they put in, either in the work or home situation. For instance, married women often provide a whole range of unpaid services for their husbands' businesses, in particular self-employed men. Such men:

> ... can be heavily dependent upon their wives' effort for undertaking a wide range of clerical and administrative duties. Accordingly, these married women are often forced to give up their paid jobs and to abandon their careers in order to under-write the efforts of their 'self-made' husbands.[3]

Is this another example of women's generosity of spirit? Not only do they give up their own career aspirations, but they also work unpaid. A women friend of mine did the administrative work for her partner's struggling business, only to be left to bring up the children on her own when it finally got off the ground. Quite a shock emotionally, and disastrous financially. Her assumptions about the future had not taken such a possibility into account but one in three marriages do end, and women with children may not seem like a viable option for another eligible partner!

We can't legislate for what the future will bring, but we can protect ourselves from joining the ranks of the new poor by making the most of our income-generating potential now. This means serious planning, creating new chances, and making the most of any opportunities that come along.

Life and career planning has been a regular feature of my own life and I have periodically taken time out to go through the exercises presented in the second half of this chapter. It really helped to review what I was doing, how I felt about it, and where I wanted to go in the future. My first experience of needing to stop, reflect and change direction occurred upon leaving school at sixteen. I had followed my mother's advice and enrolled on a secretarial course when it suddenly dawned on me that working in an office, doing mindless repetitive work, at a low wage, might be my lot for years to come. Life had to be better than that! I wasn't sure what my options might be, but nothing about the lives of my mother's generation appealed to me. Most worked in poorly paid jobs in oppressive settings, and had endless domestic responsibilities and chores at the end of a long working day. None of them seemed particularly happy or fulfilled, either at home or work; they all looked rather harassed and stressed.

Having completed the training I worked as an au-pair in

Germany and Italy for a year, and explored what other options might be available. Even then I knew myself well enough to realize how much I wanted financial independence in order to feel okay about myself, but wasn't sure how to achieve this on my current skills and qualifications. I reckoned that having a couple of languages would come in handy whatever happened, and maybe living in a foreign culture would provide more insights into the possibilities open to me. This time away challenged a lot of assumptions I had about myself and 'my rights', particularly by meeting with and talking to other young people who had a much stronger sense of what they wanted and were 'going for it'. I eventually realized that I needed to devote more time to getting properly trained and qualified, and that this would provide me with the basic ingredients for greater career choice, job satisfaction, and income generation.

As a result I went back to college, took 'A' levels, then went on to University and finally obtained post-graduate qualifications. It was a long haul, and I sometimes lost track of what I was trying to achieve. At times the costs seemed too high given the fun my contemporaries were having spending their salaries. Somewhere, however, I knew my life opportunities had to be enhanced by the experiences, knowledge and qualifications I was gaining.

Fortunately, now I am in my forties, I am reaping the rewards of earlier years of hardship. I have far more options as a result of professional qualifications, and have greater power to determine my work pattern and income level. I work for myself, respect my need to balance work and non-work activities, and can buy in support for my responsibilities at home and work. So take heart; anything is possible if you want it enough. Allow yourself to dream a little, to have a vision of what you want out of your life, and then put effort into making it happen. You have the right to a lifestyle which values and enhances you; you are worth more than your upbringing and conditioning might suggest.

MAKING A START

The process of planning your future may seem rather alien at first, for we are rarely encouraged to plan or think about our lives independently. It is important that you start to take yourself seriously and give yourself permission to plan your future. You won't always have the responsibilities you have now – being the mother of dependent children, looking after an ageing parent – so what options do you want to make available in the future?

It is easy to assume we will be rewarded for working hard, but unfortunately the nature of organizational life is such that getting noticed demands a sensitivity to, and willingness to play, organizational games. We shall speak more of this later (see page 134); being seen to excel at the 'right thing' is often valued more than doing most things well. To succeed up the organizational ladder requires clarity about goals and strategies, and creating supportive networks and mentors. Before you take this route (which means adopting the male model of success) take some time to look at what you really want, where you would ideally like to go in your life, and what would give you satisfaction. Maybe it's getting out of the 'rat race', rather than learning to be a better rat! Begin to reduce your stress and really look after yourself by working through the life and career planning exercises. You may be surprised and delighted by the results.

WHAT DO WE REALLY WANT?

Life and career planning is about giving yourself the time to reflect upon your life so far, and starting to imagine the type of life and career you want. For example, some of the choices could include:

* Whether to progress whole-heartedly with our careers, or have a child.
* Whether to make sacrifices and follow our partner in her/his career.
* Whether finally to leave an unsatisfactory job or relationship.
* Whether to confront higher management about discriminatory practices.
* Whether to take a trip of a lifetime now, or put it off yet again.
* Whether to stop work, and return to full-time education.
* Whether to work full-time, part-time, or job-share.
* How long to take off after childbirth.
* How to manage a career break.
* What qualifications to go for to secure a better paid future.
* How much pension to go for to secure a comfortable retirement.
* How to combine work with family obligations and responsibilities.

Such decisions are difficult, but have a go at confronting the process head-on by working your way through the following exercises. They have been presented so as to allow you to explore who you are and then to identify what you want out of your life, and it is a good idea to work through them at regular intervals. I try to complete these exercises about once every twelve months as it enables me to reassess what I am doing and how it matches my plans for the future.

PLANNING EXERCISES

Present life

Here are some questions to help you start thinking about your present life. Find a quiet place and take about ten to fifteen minutes answering them. Be as honest and thorough as you can — it's *your* life we are talking about!

1. Describe, very briefly, your personal and work life today. To what extent are you satisfied with your personal life?
2. What is changing in your life?
   In your work?
   In your personal life?
3. What are the changes you would like to make in your life?
   In your work?
   In your personal life?

So, any surprises? How did you rate your satisfaction with your life, and where are the major areas of dissatisfaction? What important pieces of information has this exercise given you about your ability to assert yourself in certain key situations? Are you experiencing any major stresses, and what are the implications for looking after yourself better? Do you need to use some of the assertion and time-management techniques? Are you going through any major transitions, such as starting a new job, having a difficult time in your relationships, having a baby, losing a parent or a much-loved friend, or getting separated or divorced? What are the implications in terms of looking after yourself, and what do you think you need to do to make your work and personal life more satisfying?

Jot down any new thoughts, and then put them to one side. Having explored some of the major experiences and changes you are going through at the moment, we shall now move on to explore important experiences and relationships you have had in your life and see what common themes we can identify. This will help you to have greater clarity about the values, experiences and people that you hold dear.

Self-disclosure

Write down the first thing that comes into your head when you read through the next five questions.

1. What was the high point of your week, last week?
2. Who is the one individual who is most responsible for making you the person you are today?
3. What was the most risky decision you ever made?
4. Who do you admire most?
5. If you were suddenly told you had only six months to live what would you do in that time?

Just stop and read through your answers a couple of times and see if you can recognize any common themes. For instance, was the high spot at work or at home? Where are you getting most fulfilment? What does it take to make you feel happy, and how often are you able to experience this at work or home? For instance, if I was to complete question number one, I would have to say that the high spot of last week was meeting a friend for a drink and meal, and having the time to share what was going on for both of us. It felt quite therapeutic to have all that time exchanging news and information, and having someone give me really good attention. This tells me how much I need to build in times with friends and not to let work dominate so much.

So, if these answers are significant events and people, what changes does this indicate? What would be the costs, and are you willing to pay them? Perhaps you need to think about changing your job, or leaving an unsatisfactory relationship? What do you need in your life, and are you getting it now? How could you get more of it in the future, what would you need to prioritize? At this stage it might help to share any insights you are gaining with a friend and see what thoughts they have.

The next step is to have an overview of our life to date, to provide insights into the impact of significant events and how we have coped.

Lifeline

Find a large piece paper, and on it draw a line which represents your life so far, indicating the significant experiences and transitions, the people and events that were/are significant in making your life what it is today. Start with your birth and work up to the present point in time. When you have finished this line, find a different coloured pen and draw a second line, which corresponds to the first, but which indicates the emotional highs and lows you have experienced. Take 15 minutes to do this. Having completed both parts of the task, meditate on your lifeline and focus on the following questions.

1. Where have you made significant decisions about your work or personal life?
2. Where have you just drifted?
3. What patterns or trends are there in your lifeline?
4. Did you consider other people in your lifeline?
5. How have these people affected you?
6. How do you feel about your past life experiences and the 'you' who lived them?

Again, what has doing this exercise told you, or reminded you, about yourself? What has made you the person you are, and what of your past and present life do you want to take into the future? When I do this exercise I am reminded of people who have been instrumental in helping me change and develop. For instance, important relationships with teachers at school, and college, who were encouraging and supportive; the challenge of working abroad; taking a leap of faith into a new job or relationship; friends and family members who have been loyal during the hard times; the pain of loss, through death, or separation; and the joy of new sights, sounds and experiences. All of these have had a profound effect on my life and in shaping who I now am. This knowledge helps to remind me of what I value and want to take forward, and what it may now be time to let go of.

In order to help you to further identify what you value and

want to take into the future, work quickly through the following questionnaire, and see what strikes you as important.

Life questionnaire

1. *What is important in your life?* Rate these items on a scale of 1–3 (1 being high and 3 being low).

   * a loving relationship
   * being attractive
   * a satisfying marriage/partnership
   * long holidays
   * being creative
   * having an impact on the world
   * opportunity to make your own decisions
   * a beautiful home
   * good health
   * travel
   * friends
   * a good sex life
   * lots of books
   * world peace
   * being treated fairly
   * confidence
   * influence and power in your community
   * spirituality
   * religion
   * someone who needs you
   * someone to take care of
   * order
   * a closeknit family
   * other

2. *What is important at work?* (1–3)

   * to work alone
   * regular hours and guaranteed pay
   * totally unstructured work-day
   * self-employment
   * good supervision
   * having a variety of tasks
   * working in a small organization
   * little responsibility and risks

* short travelling time
* other

3. *Choose 3 things from the list below that gives you the most satisfaction in your work.*

   * to be excited by what you're doing
   * to help others solve problems
   * to contribute to society with worthwhile work
   * to be recognized as an authority
   * to motivate yourself
   * to work things out
   * to work within a structure
   * to find new solutions
   * to have a choice of time
   * to make a lot of money
   * to work in a team
   * to work outside
   * to be respected for your work
   * other

Personal aims and goals

Ask yourself the following questions

1. What don't you want from your life?
2. What should you want according to the significant people in your life?
3. What have you always wanted to do some day?
4. What would you do if you could do anything you wanted for a year?
5. How much money would you like to be earning in a year?

How are your personal aims different from your present reality?

* Have I really gone for what I want
* Are my goals based on pure fantasy?
* Are they achievable?
* Are they life-enhancing?
* Do they hurt anybody?
* Are they legal?
* Are they good for all concerned?
* Can I see myself as already having them?
* Am I willing to undertake any difficulties associated?

* Can I handle the rewards associated with achieving them?
* Am I willing to take any responsibilities associated?

(Adapted from *Prospering Woman* by Ruth Ross.)

Having gained some new insights, find a second sheet of paper and sketch out what you would like the rest of your lifeline to look like. Pinpoint the year of your death, and then fill in the years between. If I were doing my lifeline I would like to consolidate my career over the next five years; to have moved away from training into consultancy, research and writing, be more settled in my life and working part-time. From forty-five to fifty, I intend to be working and living abroad for large parts of the year. I will have gone on a world tour before I am fifty. At that age, I shall live in the country, in semi-retirement, writing novels and enjoying a full and satisfying emotional and social life. So, how about you, what do you want? Give it a go! Spend as long as you like reaching decisions that make sense for you and the life you would like to be leading.

When you are working through the lifeline consider the following if it helps to give it some structure; ignore it if it restricts your creativity. Feel free to use lots of different coloured pens and symbols.

Consider the following
* significant changes in family relationships
* when work patterns change
* when you retire
* where you would ideally like to live
* when the children will be leaving home
* what significant relations begin and end
* what you accomplish
* what your life will have meant to others
* what you want included as essential
* how you want to be spending your last years of life

Having achieved a sense of the shape of your future life, put the book down for a while, and think about what you have discovered. You may choose to change aspects of your lifeline when you have had time to reflect, but at this point you deserve a break; creating your lifeline can be quite taxing emotionally. Whatever happens, though, don't forget to keep checking out what you've written. I have kept all the lifelines I have completed over the years, and my projections and predictions into the future have usually come true. Nancy Paul, in her book, *Developing Personal Effectiveness — A course for women*, from which some of the above exercises are modified, writes that 'People who plan achieve over 95 per cent of their goals'; so, we can achieve our ambitions if we plan and act accordingly. Similarly, Ruth Ross in *Prospering Woman, A Guide to Achieving the Full, Abundant Life*, feels we need to allow ourselves to want, and that, 'wants are thoughts, and thoughts are creative power'. Make sure, therefore, that your life projections represent what you *really* want.

Try working through the next exercises when you feel a little stuck about what you are doing and where you are going. When you feel the need to relax, and contemplate doing the relaxation technique already identified, you might like to take some time working through the stages of 'My ideal future'.

My ideal future

Imagine yourself ten years from now. How will you look? What type of clothes will you be wearing? What type of work/non-work activities will you be involved in?

Think carefully about your answers to the following questions:

1. Where will you be living? Imagine where it is and what it looks like; how is it furnished, equipped, decorated? Is there a garden?
2. Where will you be working? Imagine where it is. What does the place look like?
3. How will you be spending you non-work time? How much non-work time will there be?
4. How much money do you earn, and how do you spend your income?
5. How much time will you have left to do the things you really want to? What are they?

Having completed the exercise, jot down anything of significance, and then refer back to your lifeline. How does the 'ideal future' exercise match up with the lifeline? Are there any changes you need to make to the lifeline in the light of more recent thoughts and dreams? If this is what you want, you need to think about how you are going to achieve it. What actions are you going to take in order to make the present move towards the future? Again, does it entail being clearer and more assertive in your relationships with

	Year 1	*Year 2*	*Year 5*	*Year 10*
Home Life				
Work Life				
Relations				
Finance				
Leisure				

others at home and at work? Do you need to change jobs, or ask for a pay rise? Do you need to put your house on the market, or buy your first home. Do you need to review your responsibilities, and think about letting some of them go? Remember, you have a right to decline responsibility for other people's problems. If a relationship is dead, isn't it kinder to all concerned to admit to this and let it go, rather than hanging on in the hope it will eventually get better? Face up to it, deal with the ending, and let go. Do you need to think about managing your time better in the present and short term to start the process of achieving your ideal? As always it is up to you, but life will be less stressful if you are honest to yourself and others about who you are and what you want.

Another way of ordering the same material is to think in terms of what you would ideally like to be doing in one, two, five and ten years time. Think about each year in terms of what you would want from your home life, work life, your significant relationships, financial matters and leisure activities. How you keep yourself fit, healthy and happy.

Before moving on to look at specific actions you need to take in the very short term to achieve your life goals, how about reflecting on the multitude of skills and talents you have now. Our lack of assertion can mean that we undervalue ourselves, so try a little boasting; it will help compensate for all the times you have denied yourself the pleasure of celebrating your successes. Take a large sheet of paper and jot down everything that you know you can do, from communicating and listening to driving, cooking, managing your time, and asserting yourself.

Having completed the list, what is missing? What do you need to focus on in order to achieve your desired lifestyle?

1. What additional skills do you need?
2. What additional training do you need?
3. What work/life experiences do you need?
4. What do others need to do on your behalf?
5. What could your workplace help with?
6. What could your friends and family help you with?

Finally, think about creating a visualization notebook. Much of what we have covered so far involves words rather than pictures, images and symbols. Allow you 'right brain', the more creative side of your brain, to give energy to your future!

* Start by collecting symbols of what you want to create in your life. These can be photos, pictures, sayings, statements, and so on, all of which have a meaning for you.
* Use at least one page for each of your key life areas.
* Paste a picture of yourself in the middle of the page, and surround it with appropriate symbols and colours.
* Label each page with a goal for the future.

Then try visualizing your goals. Find a time when you are feeling calm and positive, and a place where you won't be disturbed.

* Relax your body by going through some breathing and relaxation stretches, and clear your mind of any worries.
* Take some deep breaths, feeling more and more relaxed.
* Glance at the pages in your notebook; put them to one side and focus on your breathing.
* Then recall your chosen goal for the day.
* Allow images of achieving your given goal to form in your mind. Visualize each detail in a dreamlike state. Breathe deeply and ask yourself how it would feel if you already achieved your goal.
* Stay in this picture until you see yourself acting successfully.
* Visualize an entire day being your ideal self.

* Complete the exercise by focusing back on your breathing, and allowing yourself to come around slowly.

(Adapted from *Prospering Woman* by Ruth Ross.)

BECOMING MORE PROSPEROUS

Ruth Ross has identified 'nine steps to prosperity'. This prosperity is defined by you; it does not refer only to material prosperity (although this alone would be of great benefit for many of those women living on or below the poverty line). However, the nine steps she suggests provide a overview of the processes we need to address in order to be really 'prosperous' in our lives.

Step 1: Law of self-awareness
When we know who we are and what we want, we can have what we want in life.

Step 2: Law of wanting
Experiencing choice means knowing what we want and why we want it.

Step 3: Law of planning
Without planning there is no consistent prosperity.

Step 4: Law of releasing
We must get rid of what we don't want to make room for what we do.

Step 5: Law of compensation
There is a price for everything and we always pay.

Step 6: Law of attraction
We attract what we are.

Step 7: Law of visualization
We become what we imagine, positive or negative.

Step 8: Law of affirmation
We become what we want to be by believing and affirming that we already are it.

Step 9: Law of loving
Whatever we want for ourselves we must also desire for others.

These steps put our life and career planning into context; each step confirms something we already know, if only we will listen to our *inner knowing*, which is gained from a real understanding of ourselves and who we are as individuals. To what extent have you started tapping into your intuition based on self-knowledge? If you have begun to do this you are on the way to becoming a prosperous woman.

Next we move on to exploring the issues of sexuality, the menopause, and working with the environment. Whilst reading through these next chapters don't forget to bear in mind what you want from the future so that you know what to pay attention to in the present. Good luck!

5

Sexuality

Considering that organizations have, until quite recently, been structured to meet the needs of men, to what extent is it possible for women to feel comfortable with their sexuality at work? And if, as is suggested in *The Sexuality of Organization*,[1] men and women spend considerable time thinking and worrying about sex, what concerns do women have, and how adequately are they dealt with in the workplace? The authors of this book suggest that sexuality is seen as 'frightening, uncontrollable, illegitimate, unpredictable, chaotic', in part due to the belief system of the Judaeo-Christian tradition. If this is true, how possible is it for anyone to feel good about their sexuality, let alone women, one of whom was deemed responsible for man's fall from grace!

The reality for many women, however, is that they have to trade on their sexuality in order to be acceptable for many jobs. The occupations normally available to women tend to focus as much upon their physical attributes as their competence: jobs such as reception and secretarial work, shop assistant, and airline hostess, to name but a few. In many cases women have been marginalized into areas of work which have tended to reinforce stereotypical behaviour, which accounts for their predominance in the service sector in support roles.

It does seem that it is increasingly difficult for women to feel good about themselves as they get older. Helen, a secretary, writes:

Lately I've started having really bad periods which make me feel sick. I don't feel I can mention it in the office; the men wouldn't like it. They would be very embarrassed; they don't like me to remind them that I am 52. I feel an enormous pressure to keep looking young. They really wouldn't like it if I allowed myself to go grey and get fat. There are secretaries here who look older than me and the men don't remember their names. People joke about it, but it's really very serious underneath.[2]

Although women are in a stronger position at work today, by virtue of numbers, changes in legislation around equal pay and opportunities, and an increased willingness on the part of some organizations to confront behaviour deemed sexist, there is still a long way to go. In particular women need to start asserting their rights in relation to the role of sexuality in the workplace; they need to develop their own standards regarding acceptable sexual behaviour, by assertively articulating what feels appropriate and comfortable for them.

What are some of the roles imposed on women at work? Rosabeth Moss Kanter, an American consultant, has written extensively about these[3], and the following list is based on her findings.

ROLES AT WORK

Earth Mother

The earth mother is required to perform a pseudo-therapeutic function within the organization. She tends to be receptive, rather than active, the listener rather than the doer. She tends to be used, but rarely noticed, by the organization.

Pet

The pet is the mascot of the organization, expected to stay on the sidelines and contribute very little. She is patronized, undermined and undervalued. She may be made a fuss of, but is rarely taken seriously.

Seductress

The seductress is viewed as a sexual object, and although admired is rarely treated with respect. She may experience actual or borderline sexual harassment and is the subject of considerable gossip. Although noticed, she is rarely attributed with having any skills or talent.

Iron Maiden

Women who reject the above roles may find themselves labelled as 'militant feminist' or 'iron maiden' or 'man-hater'. Such women are noticed, but feared more than valued.

At the same time it is suggested[4] that women may also be viewed as:

* Less serious about their job, because of other commitments.
* More sensitive than men, and likely to be diverted from tasks by interpersonal issues.
* Not good at taking the initiative.
* A potential threat, because they are not 'one of the boys'.

MANAGING OUR SEXUALITY

So how should we behave in order to contradict these images, whilst at the same time being true to ourselves and our gender? How do we cope with behaviour at work which we may identify as sexually harassing? How sexual should we allow ourselves to be? Where are the boundaries, and what are the costs of over-stepping them? Unfortunately, it is usually assumed that women are responsible for managing the level of sexual intimacy in everyday encounters with males. If something goes wrong, there-fore, it must have been the woman who was at fault; been dressed inappropriately; been giving out misleading non-verbal signals; been at the wrong place at the wrong time.

How does this fit with our own experience of working in organizations? Sexuality and sexual attraction are a common feature of human interaction, and people are always noticing where sexual energy is focused. At the same time, most people enjoy flirting, and a lot of 'quasi -courtship' behaviour occurs at work, some of which develops into flings, affairs, courtships, or committed relationships. Many people meet their partners at work, and this is true for both heterosexuals and homosexuals. An estimated 10 per cent of the population is homosexual, and many now feel safer about 'coming out' in the workplace. Although many others may still feel too threatened to admit to their sexual preference, it does play an important role in their behaviour at work.

Male bonding and networking

An important concept to explore in relation to sexuality at work is the whole notion of male bonding. I have previously talked about the importance that men give to playing by the 'rules', and linked to this, is a series of organizational rituals which reinforce certain types of male behaviour. Men are allowed to be quite physical with each other, but only within certain defined limits. The works' football and rugby teams, provide the most overt examples of male intimacy and bonding, and also the 'boys' night out' with the mates, for example. These situations can often mask a mutual appreciation and attraction between many of the men, which they cannot express openly for fear of censure.

It is important to realize that men working in an organization can be operating from a position of fear, in just the same way as women new to the world of work. Men do not feel that organizations are places of safety either, but are able to manoeuvre themselves around more skilfully by knowing the 'rules', developing 'safe' networks and watching their backs. Many fear intimacy, however, in case they become vulnerable to more devious or skilful counter-attacks. Thus they may feel unable openly to admit their warmth and affection for each other, preferring instead to engage in teasing and 'horseplay'. Women may therefore frighten some men, and cause them to attack from this position of fear. Some may fear disruption to the 'natural order of things', the imposition of demands for changes, or the reappearance of the all-powerful 'mother' who determined their well-being when they were at their most vulnerable. After all, wasn't work the place where men were supposed to get *away* from difficult women in their lives?

Sexist behaviour

Some men use teasing, flirting and harassment as a way of keeping women 'in their place'. Their way of dealing with 'uppity' women is to focus attention on their attributes and rating as sexually desirable or otherwise. Thus some male behaviour can be quite offensive, and this applies to both the teenager working as an office junior and to the mature woman returning to work after bringing up a family. Many men will as readily comment upon an older woman's attractiveness, or lack of it, as that of a younger one. They feel as though they have the right to define a woman's sexual desirability by their thoughts, attitudes and behaviour. All women regardless of age, race and sexual preference, are vulnerable to such assumptions.

The experience of many women would suggest that a lot of men really don't know how to work with them. These men cope with this problem by putting a woman into one of a number of categories, including those already identified, thus excluding her from male groupings. Others cope by resorting to sexist behaviour, whereby the acceptable behaviour is that manifested by the white heterosexual male. They then feel that they are the winners (an important concept for many men in the workplace) and all others, in particular women, black or disabled people, are the losers. Sexual harassment − sexism at work − can be viewed, therefore as a manifestation of men's assumed right to impose their will on less powerful women in the organization.

We know that things are changing, but until organizational cultures are more women-friendly, women will need to think carefully about how to manage their sexuality. Consider the following key issues:

* How to relate to male colleagues, bosses or staff.
* How a friendship with a male colleague or boss will be interpreted.
* How to challenge office gossip if it arises.
* How to assess the extent to which it may be safe to come out as a lesbian.

Relationships at work

Friendships and relationships are a part of working life, and some of these may become sexual. The existence of organizational hierarchies can create situations in which those at the top, usually white men, may appear more attractive than they actually are. Thus 'romantic liaisons' occur, often between the more powerful male and the less powerful female. If and when these fade out the woman frequently experiences more organizational censure than the man. In the most extreme cases, the woman has been forced to move within the organization, or leave, whereas the man may experience no such disruption. Thus women need to be clear about the possible consequences of their behaviour on both their work reputation and career prospects.

Romantic liaisons are often viewed as problems because they can upset the power dynamics within an organization. The junior woman can obtain more power by virtue of her association, making others feel disturbed, angry, resentful or jealous. It may also result in both parties being less efficient at work, and it can affect communication and lower morale. Women need to be acutely sensitive to these issues or they could be passed over for promotion because of some perceived minor indiscretion. What is okay for the boys – in that they are allowed to 'kiss and run' – is *not* okay for the girls.

This means that womens' survival in the organization necessitates an awareness of the impact of their sexuality and a willingness to modify dress, actions and non-verbal communication if they seem inappropriate to life/work goals. This may mean:

* Getting advice and feedback on your appearance and what image you project through your clothes. You may need to change your image at work, and not over emphasize your sexuality, at the expense of your skills and competence.

* Getting feedback on your verbal and non-verbal communication and ways in which you could conduct yourself in a more 'professional' manner within the workplace.

* Being prepared to assert yourself, immediately, in certain ambiguous situations, so that other people don't get the wrong idea.

* Confronting any sexist behaviour, sexual harassment and sexual innuendo as and when it occurs.

* Making and maintaining clear boundaries with colleagues and higher management. Maybe you can't afford to take the risk that other people might misinterpret a friendly luncheon date as something more 'intimate'.

Deborah L. Sheppard conducted a series of in-depth interviews with thirty-four women in managerial and professional positions.[5] Her findings reinforce the contention that woman have to learn to manage their sexuality and gender in order to be accepted in the organization. They have to appear both 'feminine' and 'businesslike' at the same time.

Without constant vigilance regarding gender (and sexual) self-presentation, these women perceive that they run the risk of not being taken seriously, not being heard, and not receiving necessary information – in other words, of not being able to participate fully in the organizational system.

Some of the women coped by 'blending in' to the existing organizational culture. This meant 'feminine' in terms of appearance, yet 'businesslike' in behaviour, which included being seen as rational, competent, instrumental, impersonal – in other words, stereotypically masculine. They expressed a concern for appearing too feminine or too masculine because it would mean a loss of credibility. They mentioned the care they took in dressing for work in order to convey an image as 'serious' managers. Hair colour and style, amount of make-up and jewellery, were all seen as important in managing their self-presentation, and many of them claimed it was better to 'err on the side of conservatism'. They mentioned, for instance, the value of the padded suit-shoulders, wearing understated colours, and tailored conservative styling.

> ... when I don't want anyone to think I'm a woman, you know, when I just want to be part of the woodwork ... I wear this beige suit with a white blouse and it's very well cut and it looks expensive, and I look appropriate and it's perfect, it's great. I just fade right away ...[6]

These techniques of desexualization were also related to organizational status, in that there was a perceived need for women managers to establish a difference between themselves and women secretaries or administrative staff in order to be taken seriously. One woman wears suits and blouses with long sleeves and high necks in order to 'do nothing to provoke or to play on my sexuality ... I enjoy being a woman but I don't want to use it'.[7] Other women de-emphasized their breasts by wearing high-necked blouses, avoiding sweaters, and wearing tailored jackets. There was general acceptance of the need to create an appearance of wealth and status in order to convey authority and power. In one writer's view '... dressing to succeed in business, and dressing to be sexually attractive, are almost mutually exclusive'.[8]

Dealing with pregnancy and children is another important area to consider. Pregnant women are rarely seen as powerful, and mothers' of young children are deemed as less committed to organizational goals than single or older women. We must confront this stereotyping and not allow organizations to dismiss us for choosing to be a parent as well as a worker. Men have always seen themselves as having this right.

It is not our world, the world of work; we did not make the rules, and until we have greater access to organizational power, we need to tread lightly and make our decisions carefully. Women's behaviour at work is under the microscope, and open to censure from those in powerful positions. We must therefore ensure our behaviour is not open to misinterpretation, for rumours can ruin a women's self-esteem and career, as will be seen on the following pages.

SEXUAL HARASSMENT

Sexual harassment, although only recently acknowledged as an issue for working women, has been a source of considerable distress for many in the past. Some men have used it as a means of keeping women 'in their place', whilst others have colluded by not trying to prevent it.

According to one definition 'sexual harassment is merely sexism in a specific location, the workplace'.[9] It includes 'unwanted and intrusive male behaviour, of whatever kind, forced on women ... whether in the form of uninvited sexual advances or of demands for time, attention and sympathy. Sexual harassment can be understood as part of a continuum of sexist behaviour, whereby the men concerned feel totally justified in forcing what they want on non-consenting women. This can include intrusions into a woman's thoughts, behaviour, space, time, energy or body.[10] As already noted such male behaviour is so familiar that most women assume it is something that they have to put up with in a work situation.

As we get older most of us develop strategies for coping, which although moderately effective can mean having to limit our options and potential. For instance, we are sensitive to non-verbal communication, and strive to refrain from sending out any ambiguous messages regarding our 'availability'. It is almost as though some men will assume we are available unless we make it very clear that we are not. Again, a women's skill in doing this will often depend on her assertive powers. If a senior male starts to become too familiar, how do we protect our space, save face, and keep our jobs? Where is the boundary between friendship, harmless flirtation, and harassment? The boundary needs to be what is acceptable to the individual. We need to make it absolutely clear that we do not want certain assumptions, comments or actions directed our way. A non-assertive woman who is harassed may experience enormous guilt, assuming that the incident must have been her fault in some way. Whilst it is always important to acknowledge appropriate responsibility for any situation, we must realize how organizations give men the permission to ignore or misinterpret our signals, behaviour or words, especially if they are in a position of power or authority.

In recent years attention has been focused on the amount of 'bullying' which goes on in organizations. On a radio programme in 1990 men and women talked about the distress caused by their overwhelming sense of powerlessness to challenge the boss who was systematically bullying them. Examples ranged from head teacher bullying junior staff to supervisors bullying trainees. Sexual harassment seems to be part of that continuum; those in power show little respect for the needs and boundaries of those without. Bosses can be aggressive in their behaviour by not respecting the rights of other people. Whilst less powerful men can also experience this, women tend to be at the bottom of the power base, and often assume that they have to put up with bullying and harassment, or get out.

Coping and surviving

So, if harassment is a part of both the work culture and the wider culture, how have women survived? It seems essential that women develop a definite sense of their right to space, maintain a clear and firm eye-contact if and when necessary, and do not convey a coyness either in terms of overall body posture or facial expression.

One of the situations I have to cope with frequently is staying in hotels alone. Any woman in this position is the object of much attention; you are assumed to be up to no good, and the more expensive the hotel the more oppressive these attitudes can be. It helps to be well dressed, but this doesn't prevent staff or guests treating you as though you have no right to be there, and as if you are not worthy of good service. One can therefore be ignored by waiters at the breakfast table, and hurried out of the dining room by over-attentive staff. Taking something to read can help, but sometimes I have had a meal sent to my room rather than have to eat alone and cope with the attention or inattention of others.

After a long day at work I don't feel up to coping with yet more aggressive behaviour.

Whilst many women suffer from some form of harassment, black and Asian women are often subjected to even greater degrees of sexual harassment. In the USA black women are treated as even more publicly available to men than white women. In the case of women of colour, the experience of racism and sexism go hand-in-hand. Any woman, however, will find sexual harassment stressful; it may result in deteriorating health or absenteeism, and she may choose to leave her job rather than create a fuss. Once again, the woman suffers, and the organization loses an important resource.

Until quite recently, men quite literally got away with it because they were seen as a more valuable resource to the organization. Undoubtedly, they went on to bully and harass other women. This was a common complaint from women in the London borough where I did some recent development work. Most of the difficulties these women had at work were related to the aggressive behaviour of their male bosses.

Finally, systematic sexual harassment has been reported as a strategy for keeping women out of male-defined organizations, such as the fire service, police force and civil engineering.

Symptoms of harassment

Women who are being harassed suffer from many of the following:

* decrease in job performance and job satisfaction
* absenteeism
* anxiety, tension, irritation, depression
* increased alcohol, cigarette and drug use
* sleeplessness and tiredness
* problems with weight and diet
* migraine
* coronary heart disease
* difficulty with family and personal relationships
* physical and mental illness

If you notice a colleague indicating any of the above, you could check out if she feels uneasy about the way her male colleagues or bosses are treating her.

As already mentioned, many women feel compelled to leave their organizations rather than confront the situation. Many feel too non-assertive to challenge those concerned, or to approach their union or management for support. In many cases members of the union or management were actually involved in the harassment and so the women felt they had no choice but to look for other work. Such action can result not only in the loss of a job/career that was valued, but also rights to promotion, sick pay, training and a pension, which are usually linked to an individual's length of service. Such moves can also feed into the notion of women as lacking commitment and being unreliable, as there may not appear to be any appropriate reason for leaving.

If women felt better about themselves and were able to assert themselves more, maybe there would be fewer incidents of sexual harassment. It does take courage to assert yourself, but how much better to cope with the initial discomfort than to leave a job that you enjoy, or lose out on promotion or a decent pension.

How widespread is harassment

According to a survey carried out by the Alfred Marks Bureau during the eighties, 60 per cent of participating employees had received unwelcome sexual attention, with 17 per cent having been harassed more than six times. Other research found that 54 per cent of women managers questioned had experienced some form of harassment, particularly women in lower- and middle-management positions.[11] Such findings reinforce the fact that sexual harassment is very common in organizations. Here is a list of the types of behaviour which are recognized as forms of harassment

1. sexual assault
2. demands for sex
3. touching and pinching
4. crude sexual remarks
5. persistant demands for dates
6. being eyed up and down
7. kissed on the cheek
8. flirting and sexual jokes

Its definition is as follows:

Sexual harassment happens when one person exercises power

inauthentically over another in the workplace. It involves repeated, unreciprocated and unwelcome comments, looks, jokes, suggestions or physical contact that might threaten a person's job security or create a stressful or intimidating working environment. Physical contact can range from touching and pinching, through to rape.[12]

The term includes all those actions and practices by a person, or a group of people, at work which are directed at one or more workers and which:

* are repeated and unwanted
* may be deliberate or done unconsciously
* may cause humiliation, offence or distress, and effect physical and mental well-being
* may interfere with job performance or create an unpleasant working environment
* comprise remarks, actions or literature associated with a person's sex, sexual preference or sexuality
* emphasize a person's sexuality over their role as a worker

What such research findings suggest is that:

* A large number of workers are recipients of sexual harassment at work.
* Almost all recipients are women, and the harassers are men.
* A wide range of behaviour is identified by women workers as harassment.
* The way workers view the problem of sexual harassment depends on their own awareness and experience of the issue.
* Lower management are more aware of the problem than higher management, and neither seem particularly concerned.
* Harassment by a supervisor is viewed as more serious than by a co-worker.

How do the recipients of sexual harassment feel?

What do the research findings tell us about the experiences of the recipients of sexual harassment? It would appear that many are reluctant to speak out for fear of public humiliation and retaliation at work. Many women felt they would be victimized or marginalized for objecting. For example, sexual remarks, jokes, catcalls, whistling, and teasing are commonplace at work, but these can be distressing and demeaning, and serve to remind women that they are judged primarily by their looks and sexual attractiveness rather than by their talents and skills.

For instance:

> My boss is incapable of having a meeting or discussion with me without some comment about my sex. There are constant references to the fact 'you are a woman', 'your dress', and so on, and remarks such as 'you're looking attractive today' or 'I know you will be able to influence so-and-so by fluttering your eyelashes.' I try to ignore it.[13]

> I felt humiliated every time I came into work and saw this picture of a women with her legs wide open, looking passive and provocative. I felt it reflected on me, my work status, even my ability to do my job.[14]

Many women fear that by resisting sexual harassment they could provoke violent assault or rape. Others may feel guilty about their reactions to behaviour which other people (men) consider trivial. Many are ashamed to tell anyone in case they are blamed for encouraging the harasser. Fear of embarrassment and humiliation from colleagues or an employer may prevent women from speaking out. If they do, they may fear retaliation in the form of:

* verbal abuse
* non-co-operation from male co-worker
* poor personal recommendations/references
* poor job evaluation/bonus rating
* impossible performance standards
* refusal to offer overtime
* demoting or down grading
* transfer to less satisfactory work
* worsening of shift pattern/hours worked
* termination of employment

Even if sexual harassment is proved, management is often reluctant to discipline or dismiss supervisors or male workers; it is the woman who is expected to learn how to manage the situation. Women have to take responsibility for issues around sexuality rather than men being prepared to take their share. Perhaps it all comes down to the fact that men were there first, and they set the standards.

What to do about persistent harassment

What are your options if you have been, or are, experiencing sexual harassment? Is it better to confront it than to try and ignore it?

Individual Action

* taking steps to avoid harassment
* seeking support from other workers
* keeping a written record of incidents
* making a complaint of harassment

Avoiding harassment

1. Try to keep your relationship with the harasser on a professional level.
2. If asked to work late, try to arrange this when other people are working.
3. If you have to work in the same room as the harasser, leave the door open or arrange for a colleague to interrupt from time to time.
4. Avoid asking for special treatment which may make you indebted to the harasser. Try not to do personal favours.
5. Avoid talking to the harasser about your personal life. Refuse to discuss any of his personal problems.
6. Think about what you wear. Avoid giving anyone the excuse not to take you seriously.

Getting support

1. Talk with other women in your workplace. If you discover you are not alone you may want to meet regularly to talk about workplace problems and sort out ways of tackling harassment together.
2. If there is no support in work, find it outside, from friends, family, your doctor, a women's group or your partner.

Keeping a written record

Keep a diary or a notebook handy to record each incident.

* date of incident
* location
* time
* nature of incident (cover both actions and comments of the harasser)
* your response
* your feelings at the time
* the name of any witnesses

Prepare for any possible backlash by also keeping a record of your own work; note down the jobs you are asked to do and any problems which arise in completing them. Record any comments you receive about your work, particularly when you are praised for doing well. This information will be useful if the harasser tries to destroy your credibility following a complaint.

Making a complaint

You should make it very clear you do not like harassment as soon as possible.

1. Approach the harasser, taking a friend with you. Outline the occasions when you have been harassed; make it clear you want it to stop.
2. Write a letter to the harasser indicating your concerns. Keep a copy of the letter.
3. Ask someone else – manager or union representative – to write a letter.
4. Use the formal complaints/grievance procedure at work, if there is one/
5. Ask to discuss the situation with a woman manager.
6. Tell management what action you want it to take in dealing with the harasser.
7. Even if there is no formal complaints procedure, you should report your complaint to someone in writing, and keep a copy. If the harasser is your immediate boss/supervisor, speak to someone else in senior management.
8. To ensure some action is taken, tell your management you will be in touch again in a few days to find out what has happened. Take a colleague or friend with you each time to make it harder for them to renege on any agreements.

How can you help someone who is being sexually harassed?

1. Listen to what she says, and show that you believe her. Remember, all kinds of women are sexually harassed; make it clear that you don't think she is to blame for what has happened.
2. Be sensitive to the fact that the woman may need medical help or counselling. The stress of harassment can make women ill.
3. Don't do anything without the woman's consent. Treat your conversation as confidential, and only take further action with her agreement.
4. Offer support.
5. Be willing to go with the woman to ask the harasser to stop and be ready to act as a witness. Make sure the woman is never left alone with the harasser.

Read through the following case studies and see if you can suggest ways in which Sarah, Doris and Mandy could have handled their situations more assertively.

Case Study 1 – Sarah

Sarah had known right through school that she had a talent for drawing and design. In her teens she had decided to go into architecture, and she very much enjoyed the years of study which led up to her qualifying at the age of 26. Her first permanent job was with a city council architects' department, where she was involved in working with a team on a development of sheltered housing for the elderly.

From the start she had known that women were very much in the minority in her chosen career, but she had worked hard to show that she was competent, and she had easy-going relationships with her colleagues.

Her major problems began when she started carrying out inspections of work in progress on the housing development site. Knowing that she would need to climb ladders, she always took care to wear trousers and had become quite used to the occasional whistle and cat-call that greeted her when she arrived. But on this particular site the builders' shouts seemed particularly personal and made her feel acutely embarrassed in front of the site foreman and other (male) colleagues who were with her on the site visits. As well as wolf whistles, there were calls of 'What a beautiful pair' and

'Look at those knockers'. She tried to make a joke of it, and at the same time see who was calling out.

The foreman saw Sarah's embarrassment the first time it happened, and said he would speak to the men before her next visit. But the barracking went on, and she began to dread her site visits. Quite apart from her personal dislike of the remarks, she felt that her credibility as a professional was being undermined in front of her colleagues. She felt humiliated and inadequate, and started avoiding site visits, asking a colleague from the office to go in her place. She became aware that this could adversely affect her whole career: if she didn't carry out adequate inspections, she would not be doing her job properly. She felt she couldn't ask her manager to send someone else instead, as this would be asking for special treatment. She was unable to talk over her problem with any of her colleagues because all the other architects in the office were men, and she felt they would not appreciate her difficulties; the only women were the telephonist, receptionist, and two secretaries, with whom she had only a distant relationship. Her anxiety level increased until she started having frequent sick leave with headaches and colds, and she became very depressed at her inability to cope with the problem.

So what do you think are Sarah's options? How can she look after herself, be assertive and still feel able to cope with the culture of the building site? Think back over the strategies we have explored so far. Can you think of anything which would improve the situation? I remember one participant on an assertiveness training course suggesting that the only option was for Sarah to put up with it, as it was 'just life'; that was the way men were on building sites! Surely, however, women do have rights in those situations? If you were Sarah, what would you do – would you put up with the bullying or not? How assertive would you be prepared to be?

Case Study 2 – Doris

Doris was employed by the council as an administrative assistant in the Fire Service. She was in her early fifties, and had only returned to paid employment three years earlier when her marriage ended. She was pleased with the way she had been able to build a new life for herself after her divorce, and felt she had handled well her return to full-time employment after more than twenty years spent bringing up her children.

She found the work in the Fire Service interesting, although she was keenly aware of the uniform/non-uniform divide which dominated the working atmosphere. For most of the time this did not concern her too much, but the behaviour of one particular fireman caused her great anxiety.

Maurice was a large, loud-spoken man in his mid-forties. It appeared to Doris that he did not like her, but considering he hardly knew her she felt this was more because the presence of female clerical staff spoiled the 'men-only' atmosphere of the workplace, rather than anything about her personality. Maurice's hostility was generally revealed by his refusal to include her in conversations, or talk to her at all if it could be avoided. But she felt that one aspect of his behaviour was quite aggressively aimed at her — he would refuse to use the changing rooms when putting on his uniform, and would take off his civilian trousers in front of her in the office.

The first time this happened Doris apologized for being there, and tried to hide her embarrassment. Maurice's response was 'If you're going to work amongst us, this is what you've got to get used to.' After this incident she found herself cautiously looking round the room, before leaving her desk, to check that no-one was changing, and hovering outside the office door before she went in, anxious about what she might interrupt.

At first she felt that she was in the way, and tried to be inconspicuous. But gradually she realized that it was only Maurice who ever changed his trousers in front of her, and that he was deliberately choosing to embarrass and humiliate her, and her anxiety soon developed into resentment and anger at her vulnerability.

What options does Doris have? How could she assert herself with respect to Maurice and his behaviour? To whom might she talk about the problem, and what does management need to know if she takes it further? How would you feel in this situation, and what would you ideally like to happen?

You can see that the situation caused Doris considerable stress and, if she does not manage to work the situation out, may well result in her leaving a job she really likes. Doris is being non-assertive in her behaviour, and she is being bullied by Maurice. She has rights, so what are they? What is it Doris needs to know and do?

Case Study 3 – Mandy

Mandy worked as a waitress in a pizza parlour. Her basic wage was extremely low so she had to rely on tips from the clients to supplement her wages. This meant being especially nice to customers, even when they were rude or 'over friendly'.

Mandy explained:

> All the waitresses accepted that they would have to put up with behaviour they wouldn't tolerate normally. You would often get a group of men coming into the restaurant, and they would think it funny to talk about you and your body while you were serving them. Sometimes they would actually touch you. . . pinch your bottom and there was nothing you could do about it. It was really a case of grin and bear it. It would have been stupid to complain to the manager . . . he thought it was funny too.
>
> Sometimes men would be more subtle and ask you to meet them after work, or they'd hang around for ages, drinking one coffee, waiting for you to 'go off'. You could get quite worried about it on an evening shift when you were leaving after midnight. Then you'd have to ask some of the other women to share a taxi home with you.
>
> There was one particular man who used to come in regularly when I was on afternoon shift. . . he didn't do much, just eye me up and down. I hated it, but there was nothing I could do.[15]

What are Mandy's rights in this situation, and, given the behaviour of her boss, how might she assert herself? Does she have to put up with this behaviour? If she can't, is her only option to leave the job? Women working in catering are some of the most poorly paid and badly treated; what rights do they have? Does Mandy have to put up with such intimidating behaviour – could the police be involved and, if so, what support would she get?

These are three examples of sexual harassment, which many women have to put up with every day of their working lives. No wonder many women either decide to leave organizations rather than continue coping with the distress, or suffer from stress and take sick leave. None of these women seemed to have any major sources of support, and maybe this is one of the keys to making changes. Women need to support other women who are experiencing harassment; it is a collective not an individual issue.

Gradually, too, more and more men in organizations are becoming sensitive to the problem and, having developed the women's network, perhaps the next stage is to encourage relationships with supportive men who can challenge unacceptable behaviour. By no means all men harass women, and many now are prepared to stop colluding in this 'bit of fun'. Once they have become aware of what is going on, these men will do all they can to change the values and behaviours which underpin harassment at work.

6

Managing the Menopause – A Positive Approach

The menopause is also related to sexuality in the workplace and, because it doesn't directly affect men, is rarely discussed or taken seriously in a work context. But it is extremely relevant for women who may be returning to work after a career break, and who wish to continue in employment for many years to come.

In her recent book *The Change*, Germaine Greer argues that women need to be more open to accept the processes involved in the menopause, and be prepared to become fitter in order to cope with the physical changes. She decries the widespread use of Hormone Replacement Therapy (HRT), which she sees as an attempt to defy the ageing process. To a large extent she is echoing the thoughts of American writer Rosetta Reitz, and Anne Dickson and Nikki Henriques, who are all referred to throughout this chapter. They suggest that the benefits of the change are enormous, and Germaine Greer believes it marks the 'beginning of the long' gradual change from body into soul'. Menopausal women, however, are generally treated with contempt and disdain, and we must therefore be more assertive about our rights as women who must inevitably go through the menopause. Susie Orbach sums this up well:

> After menopause there can well be another thirty years of life to live; the question is how to live it with dignity and respect and create a cultural climate that will honour and value women in all their variety and in all their ages.[1]

So what are the issues a woman may experience at the time of her menopause? Here are the views of a psychotherapist quoted in an article published in the *Guardian*, October 1991 talking about her experiece of the menopause.

I felt awful about my body. I don't think it changed dramatically but to me it felt different and it put me right off sex. I didn't like not having periods. I missed the rhythm of it. I felt marked out as an older woman, in spite of the lack of obvious change.

I had friends who kept urging me to go on HRT because it would improve my skin and make me feel better. They made me feel a bit of a Luddite for not doing it, but physically I never really felt bad enough to go to a doctor. Taking hormones seemed a bit over the top for dealing with something that is really just a question of getting older. It is emotionally painful but, in the end, I have to accept my body is different. . . one of the hardest things was going through the experience alone. I had few friends of my age to discuss it with and couldn't talk to my partner about it.

It isn't that he wouldn't have listened. I just don't think he could understand.[2]

SO WHAT IS THIS EXPERIENCE CALLED MENOPAUSE?

We menstruate, on average 13 times a year, for nearly 40 years, and we manage this monthly flow of blood in the context of both our work and personal/home environments without too much disruption to either. Very few men have an understanding of the amount of thought and pre-planning that goes into making sure that it is 'business as usual'! In fact most of us maintain normal levels of productivity, whilst suffering, at times, considerable amounts of discomfort and irritation. Menopause is treated in a similar fashion; something women just have to get on with, usually on their own, and certainly without too much disruption to either their personal or professional lives.

In the opinion of the writer Isaac Asimov, 'It is a condition that is all the more frustrating to women in that its existence is either unsympathetically dismissed by men or completely ignored'.[3] Finding a voice at work may mean sharing our experiences and having them valued, and this means talking about menstruation and menopause. In particular, we need to ensure that we have as positive an experience of the menopause as possible; the menopause isn't always stressful, but our lack of knowledge of it can be. Men's attitudes to it can be distressing, especially if we are made to feel 'invisible' or 'worthless' by being categorized as 'past it' in terms of both our sexuality and our career prospects. An example of this is the 1990 sacking of media women around the age of 50. There are very few women of this age in prominent positions on television but they do appear sometimes, and are often the objects of much derision in soap operas.

Much of the following material has been adapted from the excellent books *Menopause – A Positive Approach* by Rosetta Reitz and *Menopause – The Woman's View* by Anne Dickson and Nikki Henriques. These writers provide a wealth of ideas, techniques and options to help women take greater control of their bodies and their lives. The controversy surrounding the use of HRT, linking it with increased incidents of cancer and other related conditions, means that we need to be aware of the available alternatives. Menopause can be a positive experience, a time for reflection and making changes, which can lead to a greater sense of one's own worth. For many of us it provides an opportunity (sometimes the first) to start to take ourselves seriously. It is also an excellent time to do the life career planning outlined earlier.

Women must be prepared to talk about the menopause with other women: how we feel about it, and why and what is happening to our bodies. Although I am only in my early forties, I now take greater care of my diet, have reduced my intake of meat, coffee, salt and sugar, take vitamin supplements and am more conscientious about regular exercise, massage and acupuncture. I also build in regular and frequent breaks from work, if only the odd long weekend.

The menopause can be especially difficult for women who have not come to terms with any important psychological issues in their lives. It seems that any frustration a woman has with respect to not achieving can be magnified a hundredfold at this time. All women, therefore, need to address these issues, by having regular supportive meetings with their friends, joining a women's group, or having co-counselling, counselling or therapy sessions. You may also find that there is a local self-help group for women at this stage in their lives, so look out for information in your doctor's surgery, or in the local paper. The early signs of the menopause can hit women with the reality that there may only be limited time to do the things they have been putting off, and that they need to start sorting out their lives before it is too late.

The same applies physically; women who have not looked after their physical well-being may find menopause more stressful. This was certainly suggested by Rosetta Reitz who had to reduce her coffee intake, have therapy and take up exercise to cope more effectively with her symptoms. Once again, it is almost as if we need permission to look after ourselves; keep reminding yourself how often you have cared for others, and that now it is your turn! Other people will be willing to help if we assertively communicate what is going on, rather than playing the non-assertive martyr. If you don't get what you need you may well end up suffering from a stress-related illness, and having to take time off, and thus risk damaging your reputation and career prospects. Maybe it would be sensible to have another career break, or go for a job share or work from home, if the symptoms of menopause start to really get you down.

In the past many of my male colleagues have appeared outraged by the importance I and other female trainers/consultants have placed upon defining our own needs and boundaries. We stated clearly that we had no desire to abuse ourselves, physically or mentally, by becoming 'workaholics' and putting ourselves under the constant pressure they seemed to thrive on (or were addicted to). Such men often have enormous sophistication about the theory of stress management, but may have a misguided loyalty to an organization which could be exploiting them. They define their behaviour as commitment to organizational goals, but perhaps they are just unable to be assertive about their health and emotional needs? I suspect it all comes down to the fact that somewhere in the background there is a woman picking up the pieces! For some it could be a combination of their secretary and their wife.

Few men really seem to understand or appreciate the care-taking role that women play in their lives, thus enabling them to engage more fully with their careers. Some men are so accustomed to thinking that women's needs are secondary to their own that any woman who takes herself seriously may be viewed as less than female, and certainly as 'not playing according to the rules'. It isn't easy for any woman to confront these attitudes, but one way forward is to contradict them by your behaviour. If you don't want to follow your male colleagues to an early death, prompted by stress, destroy any chance you have for a satisfactory home and social life, or make your menopause more distressing than it needs to be, you need to start being clearer, and communicating that clarity. This is tied up with how assertive any woman is allowed to be in an organization. Unless you want to repeat all the mistakes your male colleagues have been making. assert yourself now. Organizations need women, and we can take more risks to ensure that our contribution is recognized and rewarded. We are much more than a convenient reserve pool of labour that can be manipulated according to the whims of the economic climate.

FACTS ABOUT THE MENOPAUSE

* Menopause takes about five years to complete itself.
* Menstruation generally stops sometime between the ages 45 and 53.
* A relatively small number of women begin menopause in their early forties, and some after 53.
* The most common age for menopause is 50.
* Some women experience premenopausal feelings for ten to fiteen years before the actual menstrual flow stops.
* There is a suggestion that heavy smokers menopause earlier; tall women, single women, and those without children later.
* Hot drinks, spicy foods, alcohol and stress may trigger a hot flush.
* Menopause occurs in one of three ways.

  1. *Abruptly*: The periods stop, with few if any symptoms.
  2. *Gradually*: The periods change by slowly diminishing in amount and length of flow. A woman may hardly notice the gradual change, for it may occur over a period of time lasting anywhere between six months and three years.
  3. *Irregularly*: By far the most common way is that the menstrual pattern becomes increasingly irregular. Flow may vary from heavy to scant. The number of days of flow may also become irregular. A single month or many may be slipped, or periods can occur within a shorter range of time than the usual cycle. A whole year can pass without a period, and the woman may then experience one or more periods.

* Many doctors feel that a woman is only safe to assume her periods are over when she has missed them for twenty-four months.
* Certain kinds of bleeding are not a normal part of the menopause and should be investigated by a doctor. These are:

  1. Haemorrhaging or flooding – which is an excessive flow of blood that is faster and heavier than a heavy period.

2. Lengthy staining – outside the menstrual periods.
3. Very frequent periods.

These irregularities may not be serious at all and may stop by themselves, but they should be closely watched and checked by a physician.

Polyps, fibroids, birth control pills and estrogen replacement therapy may be common causes of irregularity in bleeding.

Any kind of uterine bleeding when menopause is definitely over should receive medical attention.

* Although the clearest indicator of menopause is the end of the menstrual flow, a woman over 40 may stop menstruating because of reasons unrelated to menopause:

1. Because she is pregnant.
2. Because of a big stress situation in her life such as the death of someone close.
3. A move to a new residence.
4. A new job.

In such cases the woman is not menopausal. If there are no unusual circumstances and the periods stop, that is menopause.

SYMPTOMS OF THE MENOPAUSE

The most common symptoms of menopause are hot flushes, chills which often follow a hot flush, sweating and night sweats and also nervousness, irritability, excitability, and anxiety. Many women may also experience some of the following:

swelling breasts
weight gain
feeling bloated
depression
lethargy
emotional outbursts
temper tantrums
feeling fragile
crying
menstrual irregularity or disturbance
osteoporosis (bone changes)
backache
leg pains

vertigo
dizziness
palpitations
faintness
numbness
tingling
feeling of suffocation
mouth sores and swollen gums
dry mouth
momentary swallowing problems
hair loss or gain
insomnia
urinary frequency and incontinence
nausea
indigestion
lack of appetite or excessive appetite
flatulence
constipation
arthritis
freckles, skin spots and skin changes
vaginal changes − pruritis is a medical term for itching skin in
the vulva or genital region
senile vaginitis − is pruritis plus an irritating discharge which
may or may not be blood-tinged
arthralgias − pain in a joint
myalgias − pain in a muscle or muscles
formication − a sensation of small insects crawling over the skin
desquamative gingivitis − inflammation of gums with some
gum tissue loss

(Source: *Management Effectiveness for Women*, NEC, 1990.)

Many women experience depression and the following quotation
sums up the experience of many: 'I think there's a feeling of being
over the hill, being useless now − somehow you're not feeling
really worth anything.' Another woman says: 'I couldn't cope any
more with the tiredness and the depression and this in itself was
frightening, because I didn't know why I was feeling like this.' And
for another woman, it was important to be understood, 'I realized
that understanding it, and other people accepting it, made an
enormous difference. Because otherwise you feel you're going
mad.'[4]

Menopause can be a particularly difficult time in a woman's life because it can coincide with children leaving home and parents getting ill or dying. Husbands may be going through a career crisis, taking early retirement or facing redundancy, or have health problems. Many women are newly divorced (as a result of the husband's mid-life crisis). There may be teenagers still at home with attendant problems. Increasingly, with delayed parenthood, there may be children who are young (and exhausting), particularly if mother is working full-time. Parents may have senile dementia, cancer or heart problems. In short it can be a very stressful period indeed, and if a woman has a history of emotional problems she will be at risk during the menopause, especially if she has less than adequate support.

COPING WITH THE MENOPAUSE

It is useful to keep a menstrual record. Record the date of the period; the kind of flow you experienced; any symptoms; any changes in mood, appetite and energy. The value of recording is that it removes some of the uncertainty, and you can start to respect the needs of your body. So if you *know* you feel particularly fragile at certain times of the month, plan important meetings or tasks for other dates. If you *can't* avoid the meeting, look after yourself so that you can go well rested and perhaps better prepared than usual, thereby minimizing the degree of stress. Think about what you wear so that you feel both comfortable and confident; practice some of the stress reduction techniques already identified, particularly deep breathing and relaxation, and decline coffee and tea, which could make you feel more fragile.

Hot flushes

Hot flushes are harmless, pass quickly and usually last from fifteen seconds to one minute, and occasionally for two minutes. A sensation of heat floods over the face and neck and upper part of the chest. Profuse sweating follows frequently. They are like blushes, only the redness is deeper, and the heat is hotter, and some women feel hot in the head too. They usually begin when menstrual flow begins to wane, and continue after the periods have stopped.

Suggestions for coping

* Wear loose-fitting clothes when possible, or layers of clothing so that you can remove jackets or jumpers if you experience a flush.
* Wear sleeveless tops with jackets or jumpers.
* When you experience a flush, don't try to hide it; talk about it openly and assertively.
* Talk about hot flushes generally with your family, friends and co-workers. Don't feel ashamed of them.

At the time of a flush

* Sit quietly and make yourself comfortable.
* Take off outer layers of clothing — loosen any belt, unbutton any blouse at the neck.
* Take a few deep breaths.
* Take your shoes off, if possible.
* Remove any hairpins or rubber bands in your hair, if possible.

Take preventative action by having the following

* Vitamin E complex.
  About 50 per cent of women who go through menopause get hot flushes. Night sweats can be helped by taking Vitamin E.
* Vitamin C (taken at intervals through the day).
  Once the flushes have subsided, usually after a week, reduce the intake of Vitamin E.

Weight gain

This can be controlled by becoming more conscious of eating habits. Rather than going on a diet, develop a more healthy way of eating and stick to it for the rest of your life. For instance, reduce (or, better still, eliminate) red meat, sugar, caffeine and salt from your diet. Introduce more pulses, brown rice, organic foods and vegetables. A reduction in the amount of alcohol taken will help keep your weight down.

Bone changes

Because of calcium loss, the affected bones become brittle and can fracture easily. Women at risk are those with small bones, who do not exercise regularly, and who do not drink milk. Semi-skimmed

---

The Menopause Charter

* Stop and relax when you need to
* Cry when you want to
* Be angry when you need to be
* Say 'No' when you want to
* Exercise for pleasure
* Say 'yes it's my menopause', assertively
* Improve your diet
* Share you feelings with a friend

---

milk is apparently more full of calcium than ordinary milk. If you feel you may be in the high-risk group, you could take a supplement.

Emotional outbursts

Instead of being frightened by these, try to understand and respect your feelings, and find a safe place to explore them and their causes. This may be with close women friends, or in a more formal counselling or therapeutic relationship. It is just as important to take more time for yourself; nurture yourself, indulge yourself by having a massage, a Shiatsu session or a long hot bath. Build in meditation sessions, and if necessary consult a homoeopath or acupuncturist for additional help and advice. Take your feelings seriously be they anger, despair, frustration or depression, and work through them.

Build more exercise into your life, such as walking, swimming, cycling, tennis, yoga, dance or keep-fit classes. Incorporate your own exercises in your daily routine; walk up stairs rather than take a lift, use public transport rather than a car, and get off a couple of stops before you need to; walk to or from work occasionally, if the distance makes this feasible.

Watch your diet

Keep meals simple; eat more fresh fruit, salads, vegetables, skimmed milk, wheatgerm, nuts, raisins, cheese, eggs and grilled

fish, and ensure you have enough calcium, vitamins D. E,
B-Complex, C, magnesium, iron and iodine.

Foods rich in calcium
Skimmed milk, cheese, low-fat yogurt, canned salmon and sardines, dark-green leafy vegetables, peanuts, walnuts, sunflower
seeds, dried beans, tahini, wheatgerm, soya flour, dates, cauli-
flower, dried fruit.

Natural sources of Vitamin D
Butter, egg yolk, liver, margarine, shrimps, mackerel, sardines,
herring, salmon, tuna, sunlight.

Foods rich in magnesium
Bran, brazil nuts, wheatgerm, almonds, soya flour, peanuts, millet,
wholemeal flour, walnuts, oatmeal.

Foods rich in vitamins
Vitamin E: Cottonseed, corn, soya beans, safflower, wheatgerm,
coconut, peanut and olive oils, apple seeds, alfalfa, barley, peanuts,
rosehips, yeast, cabbage, spinach.

Vitamin C: Oranges, broccoli, Brussels sprouts, strawberries, cabbage, red, green and yellow peppers, new potatoes, pepper.

Vitamin B: Wheatgerm, brown rice, bran, soya flour, brewers'
yeast, asparagus, watercress, liver, kidney, spinach, chicken, kale,
whole-grain cereals, molasses, walnuts, peanuts, herring, salmon,
bananas, avocados, grapes, pears, cabbage, carrots, egg yolk, sardines, crab, oysters, cheese.

Foods rich in minerals
Iodine: Dark-green vegetables, lettuce, spinach, grated carrot, beet-
root, parsley, celery.
Iron: Liver, wheatgerm, wholemeal flour, oatmeal, unpolished rice,
parsley, prunes, carrot, raw celery, raw onions, apples, bananas,
cherries, dates, grapes, orange and lemon juices, peaches, pears,
mushrooms, honey, molasses, canned salmon, sardines, raw cabbage, lettuce, soya beans, cooked potatoes, spinach, pineapple and
tomatoes.

Mineral supplement in tablet form
Kelp, magnesium with calcium, ginseng, Royal Jelly, camomile
flower and valerian root, evening primrose oil.

Herbal treatment

Certain natural remedies help the body make its hormonal adjustment
and tone the reproductive system. The following are particularly
helpful to counteract the symptoms related to the menopause and
may be suggested by a herbalist: *Agnus castus* (chasteberry); false
unicorn root; hops; yarrow; St John's wort, and wild yam. Do consult
a qualified herbalist, however, for more detailed information and help.

Many women have found consulting a nutritionist useful in
combating some of the symptoms. One I spoke with suggested a
combination of Royal Jelly, bee pollen, flax oil, doug kwei root and
chlorrella. However, we all have different nutrional requirements,
so if you are interested make an appointment for a consultation.

Certain amino-acids have been suggested as helpful. These
include L-glutamine and L-phenylalanine, which can help with
depression and fatigue.

Aromatherapy oils and treatments can also help. An aromatic
bath, or applying essences directly to the skin, can be very therapeutic. The essences of cypress, sage, camomile, fennel, and gera-
nium in particular have the ability to help menopausal symptons.

Drinking certain herbal teas, such as black cohosh, sage, camomile and fennel, can also relieve the symptoms.

There is no one answer to managing the menopause. We all
need to understand ourselves a little better, and work out what we
either need to introduce to or reject from our lives. Have another
look at the chapters on assertion and stress management for
additional help in coping with situations at work and at home. The
menopause can be a very creative time; it is a time of transition,
and whereas we may experience some sadness at what we are
losing, perhaps we can also feel some joy about what is ahead of
us. The years to come could be richer than the years already spent;
we may be, and feel, freer and more confident. It is up to us to
create the life we want, both during and post-menopause. So
watch your physical and mental well-being, make sure you are
making the right career/life plans and the world could well open
up to you. Start making your dreams come true; believe in yourself
and your right to a full and abundant life.

Working with Men

For most of us, working in an organization means working with men. Women have to decide to what extent they are prepared to conform to the norms of these organizations, whilst at the same time remaining true to themselves and their own values. Although senior management is beginning to appreciate the needs of an increasingly diverse workforce, the atmosphere of the workplace can still resemble an exclusive, white, male club. Increasing numbers of women and people of colour are allowed to join, but only on condition they abide by the rules. 'Organizational cultures tend to be white, heterosexual and male-dominated. This is shown, for example, by emphasis on individualism, competition, clear boundaries, and control.'[1]

MALE CULTURE OF WORK

Some men feel just as alienated from the workplace as women, in that they do not share the dominant values of the organization, and yet may feel powerless to change the sexist and racist practises commonplace in many companies. However, most of them at least know how to 'play the game', and are often in a position to manipulate the rules for their own ends. Their socialization into manhood has provided them with the knowledge and skills needed to survive, if not necessarily thrive, in the culture of work. For instance, they understand the importance of being seen as good 'team' members and displaying behaviour suggesting commitment. They know how to get noticed and thus proceed up the career ladder.

How do men develop this knowledge? It has been suggested by Lever (1976)[2] that young boys learn the importance of rules and games from playing with their peer group. She noticed that boys play outside more, in larger, age-mixed groups, and that their games are longer and more competitive than those played by girls. Her research suggests that the boys seem to enjoy the legal debates as much as the game itself, and that even marginalized players participate equally in the squabbles.

These findings support earlier work[3] which discovered that boys were increasingly fascinated with the rules of the game, and with ensuring that conflicts were sorted out fairly. Girls, however, had a more 'pragmatic' attitude towards rules, and were more willing to make exceptions and to be innovative. This implies the importance men give to understanding and playing by their rules, whereas women have the capacity to be much more imaginative in problem-solving. Are many organizations aware of the qualities and skills women have to offer? Up till now, organizations have reflected the white, male way of doing things – not necessarily the best way.

The Stock Market is a classic example of the competitive male model, far removed from any understanding of the need to demonstrate a concern for others. In this ultimate 'male club', how do the women survive? Possibly by being tougher than the men? This may be acceptable to some women in the short term, but doesn't challenge male assumptions about their rights to exploit others, situations and the environment.

The difficulty for women working in organizations is that tradition suggests that the men's world is the 'real world', to which women must adapt if they wish to be considered equal. This is what equality of opportunity has come to mean for many: women proving that they are just as good as men in traditionally male occupations. There is little acceptance of the fact that women bring in their own skills which can add to, rather than detract from, the culture of work. For example, Lever's research[4] found that girls' play tended to be more co-operative, valued relationships, and encouraged sensitivity and empathy for others. Just think how much more humane and productive organizations could be if they took some of these values on board.

FEMALE VALUES

Anita Roddick, the founder and owner of The Body Shop, is a perfect example for the modern-day businesswoman, for she and her organization are very successful in terms of the male criteria of success, yet it is an organization in which female values predominate. Her company publicly acknowledges its responsibility to its staff, customers and the environment, and demonstrates this via its actions in the world. It consults and listens to its staff and customers, and takes responsibility for educating, training and empowering others, be they suppliers, producers, staff or customers. It is successful, but it does not seek to exploit others; rather it endeavours to add to the value of their lives in ways that don't harm the planet on which we all depend.

> Why are we always called naive and innocent; why aren't we just right? There are those men who tend to view The Body Shop as nothing more than an ephemeral business phenomenon, a flash in the commercial pan that will collapse and disappear even more quickly than it mushroomed around the world. They patronize our proselytizing, our environmental campaigning, our social welfare policies, our constant talk of putting love where our labour is. The big mistake they make is to equate our feminine values with weakness and inefficiency. What they do not realize is that while The Body Shop is founded on principles generally alien to mainstream business, it nonetheless operates according to strict criteria in terms of marketing and customer care and motivation and all the other elements that combine to make a successful retail business.[5]

Anita Roddick displays the female qualities of concern and respect, with an understanding and sensitivity to our interdependency, both with each other and with the planet. At the same time she is determined not to be ignored or silenced by the world of men. She asserts herself and her ideas. She manages herself in relation to others, and is respectful of time-management issues; she knows we must use our time properly if we are to make a difference to the world.

The Body Shop is an important example of what female values can achieve, and represents an important breakthrough. It is possible to be successful *and* operate from a position of integrity. At a conference on 'Business: The Leading Edge in the 1990s' at Dartington in 1990, Anita Roddick said 'We won't compromise on values'. Such strength suggests anything is possible when women allow themselves to listen to their inner knowing and act upon it. If we are not happy with the world of work, we need to take some responsibility for making it different; we need to assert our values in the workplace. If Anita Roddick can do it, so can we.

Over the past couple of decades many women have turned their backs on male-defined organizations and have set up on their own. Many of these businesses have tended to be smaller and more co-operatively based, where concern for the well-being of the individual, as well as the job, is deemed important. Many have been situated within the voluntary sector, and run by women for women, such as Womens' Aid, the Womens' Therapy Centre, and Rape Crisis Centres.

My own experience of working in an all-woman grouping, the Women's Resource and Training Group, as SAUS (School for Advanced Urban Studies), Bristol University, is a testament to the hardship involved in trying to evolve a more humane, woman-friendly way of relating organizationally. There were then so few alternatives to the accepted wisdom of male ways of organizing that enormous energy and commitment were needed to tackle the interpersonal difficulties which invariably arose. In order to survive the members had to deal with their feelings of anger, frustration, competition and envy.

Working on these issues contrasted sharply with the denial, covert competition and game playing that our male colleagues engaged in *vis-a-vis* each other and our group. We chose instead to own our feelings, working at solving them collectively. We did this by agreeing a set of ground rules for our meetings, including offering each other active and respectful listening, coupled with a willingness to challenge and confront when appropriate. We agreed that attendance at these monthly meetings was a pre-requisite for involvement at any level in the work of the group, and when we found the issues too difficult to handle collectively we hired the support of an organizational consultant who was both sympathetic to, and knowledgeable about, the task we had set ourselves. This process was essential in our struggle to find a more appropriate way of operating, but was not without its casualties.

Maybe Lever's findings suggests some of the reasons why so many women find working in male-defined organizations so dis-tressing. It will remind some of them of the painful experiences of being excluded from the boys' games as girls. Others may remember being allowed to participate, but only on the boys' terms, and never being given the opportunity of fully learning the rules of the game. For others, it may provoke memories of bemusement as to why the boys got so het up over a 'silly game'. Sadly, for many women, the world of work can still seem like a very demanding and potentially punishing game, where they are unlikely to be rewarded or valued for their qualities and skills.

If this is so, why have women remained silent for so long? Feminist research seems to suggest that the education system plays a large part in silencing women. Nancy Goldberger and her colleagues suggest that the education system does not adequately serve the needs of women students,[6] that most major educational institutions were originally 'founded by men for the education of men', and that even girls' schools and colleges have been modelled after male institutions. I have often wondered why school and educational establishments seemed such hostile places. There has also been considerable research regarding the paucity of attention young girls received at school,[7] and about why women find it so hard to achieve at school.[8]

So how does this exclusion from the boys' world affect young women? It teaches them to devalue their intuitive ways of knowing; they are taught to doubt their thoughts, experiences and feelings. According to Judi Marshall,

> Female characteristics and values, such as emotions, intuition, and interdependence, are denied legitimacy and are covertly or actively suppressed.[9]

She then goes on to say:

> As they create their individual lives in organizations women therefore encounter deep-rooted aspects of culture that devalue the characteristics that they have come either to symbolize or to carry. Living in this potentially hostile world, women often describe themselves as struggling to survive rather than thriving. This makes women often vulnerable, on guard; their competence, credibility and membership continually precarious.[10]

Other researchers suggest that young women are prone to:

* Express doubts about their intellectual competence.
* Feel alienated in academic settings.
* Experience formal education as peripheral or irrelevant to their central interests and development.
* Have difficulty in asserting their authority.
* Have difficulty in considering themselves authorities.

* Have problems expressing themselves in public.
* Have difficulties in gaining the respect of others for their minds and ideas.
* Have problems in fully utilizing their capabilities and training in the world of work.

Whilst a great deal of creative work has been taking place in many educational establishments, with teachers trying hard to confront many of the negative messages young girls and women receive about their innate ability, much of the damage has already been done in the family and is reinforced via the mass media, in particular the popular press, television and the cult figures of the world of music and films. The wider culture of the industrial countries still negates and devalues women's contribution, knowledge and skills. Most of us still live in a world which is profoundly disrespectful of female values. Goldberger and her co-writers say:

> In private and professional life, as well as in the classrroom, women often feel unheard even when they believe that they have something important to say . . . Many female students and working women are painfully aware that men succeed better than they in getting and holding the attention of others for their ideas and opinions. All women, like it or not, grow up having to deal with historically and culturally ingrained definitions of femininity and womanhood – one common theme being that women, like children, should be seen, not heard.[11]

You may think that this is an outdated notion, but the stories I heard during my recent work in a London borough, where I was engaged in a year-long development programme for women, conform very much to Goldberger's proposals. Many of the participants had been consistently undermined in the workplace, either by not having their contribution valued, or by being 'set-up' to fail by having to deal with impossibly difficult assignments or people. They were often confronted with long-standing organizational problems, and given no help in sorting them out. It was a sink-or-swim situation, and they were isolated from the support their male colleagues could count on receiving. They were consistently made to feel that it was their own fault that they were not coping, rather than helped to see the impossible position they had been placed in.

If you think back to your formative years, can you remember times when you were not heard, and your contribution not valued? What impact did this have on your self-esteem? How about more recently? Do you feel able to make suggestions and offer solutions to your male colleagues or boss? If you can, how are they received? How valued do you feel by the males at work, and what do you have to deny about yourself in order to keep them 'sweet'? What influence do your combined experiences have on your confidence to speak out, especially if it contradicts the 'perceived wisdom' of your 'elders and betters' (the dominant males in your life)?

Some of our difficulties in being heard are highlighted by the work of Deborah Tannen.[12] She claims that each sex has preferred topics; boys talk about things , while girls talk about feelings, and that each sex has its own conversational style. She says women use conversation to establish intimacy and connection – 'rapport-talk' – ask a lot of questions, and use 'maybe' frequently. They want to include others in their conversation and decision-making. On the other hand, boys are more definite and suppress doubts; they use conversation to establish status. She says men are more comfortable with 'report-talk'; talk is a way of establishing who is in control and has the power. She claims that one of the reasons why men hate asking questions is because it makes them feel inadequate in some way, whereas women often use questions to establish the intimacy of 'rapport-talk'.

Such differences have serious consequences for women in terms of how they may be viewed by men at all levels in the organization, and as the following example shows, can also be particularly damaging to their career prospects. She quotes the result of one such linguistic misunderstanding:

> ... in a medical school a female student who asked many questions got bad marks. Her male professors saw asking questions not as a sign of curiosity but as proof of the fact that she didn't know what she was supposed to know.

So, in order to gain respect in the workplace, we may need to learn to modify our style of communicating – engage less in 'rapport-talk', and more in 'report-talk'.

Years ago I remember reading that women used therapy to talk about their relationships with men, rather than exploring their own emotional difficulties. This is hardly surprising; these are the very relationships which cause women so much trouble. Men have determined the shape of the world in which women live, and have consistently tried to define women's reality. Any woman struggling to find out who she really is will need to explore how the most influential men in her life have tried to mould her self-image and her potential. This is not to deny the importance of mothering in this process, but many women of our generation will have been products of a type of mothering which over-valued the importance of the male-defined culture. Our mothers were probably trying hard to be 'their fathers' daughters', by living up to male values, rather than feeling positive about their femaleness and encouraging their daughters to value theirs as well. How many of our mothers valued their capacity to be interdependent, co-operative, receptive, intuitive, responsive, emotional, holistic, inward and sustaining? Little wonder that we have needed to reassess their value too!

We need to accept that overall our culture has been pretty dehumanizing, and to accept our responsibility in changing it, for all our sakes. Alice Miller testifies to the dehumanizing impact of our cultural straight-jacket. She says:

> We live in a culture that encourages us not to take our own suffering seriously, but rather to make light of it or even to laugh at it. What is more, this attitude is regarded as a virtue, and many people – of whom I used to be one – are proud of their lack of sensitivity towards their own fate as a child. . . . it was the child in me – condemned to silence long ago, abused, exploited, and turned to stone – who finally found her feelings and along with them her speech and told me, in pain, her story. Thus, it was my story I was telling in *The Drama of Being a Child*, and many people saw their own mirrored in it.[13]

We could all benefit from listening to the 'child' within us, to see what she has to say about our difficulty in finding our voice in the organization!

Women's ways of knowing are different, but does that necessarily make them inferior? Goldberger also writes:

> It is likely that the commonly accepted stereotype of women's thinking as emotional, intuitive and personalized has contributed to the devaluation of women's minds and contributions, particularly in Western, technologically oriented cultures that value rationalism and objectivity. It is generally assumed that

intuitive knowledge is more primitive, therefore less valuable, than so-called objective modes of knowing. In general, both men and women are taught to value what is assumed to be the objective 'male mind' and to devalue female intuition'.[14]

Having attended a conference on Intuitive Leadership in October, 1990, at Findhorn, a spiritual community in Scotland, I suspect that intuitive knowing will become highly valued in the coming decade. No doubt some men will claim it for themselves, rather than valuing women's intuition. But if intuition is now in vogue we can start respecting and articulating our intuitive ways of knowing, and find ways of supporting each other in saying the unsayable. It's risky, but perhaps our survival, and that of the planet, demand that we increasingly make known our values, feelings, thoughts and ideas.

DIFFICULTIES FOR WOMEN IN ORGANIZATIONS

Women in organizations have been systematically denied their rights, and devalued for either not knowing the rules or not being prepared to play by them. Until very recently women were only allowed to join an organization on the strict understanding that they knew their place, which at best was to be seen and not heard, and at worst to enter via the back door, and silently go about their menial tasks; as personal assistants, secretaries, typists, cleaners and cooks! After all, a women's place was to cater for and service her man's needs in the home, so why not at work as well?

I am reminded of the work of the feminist theologians, and in particular that of Sarah Maitland, Elaine Pagels and Mary Daly. It is interesting to note the extent to which modern-day corporations resemble the Judaeo–Christian model, in that we have God the 'father' at the top as the chief executive, and Christ and the Disciples one level below, corresponding to the deputy chief and his senior management team. Not one woman to be seen! At least Michele Roberts in *The Wild Girl*, and Elaine Pagels in *The Gnostic Gospels*, provide evidence of the role and importance of women, particularly that of Mary Magdalene in the life of Christ. They suggest that the gospels according to Paul may contain some important omissions about the role of women in the emerging band of dissidents. If this is so, why did Paul and his followers feel the need to re-write history? And why, indeed, have men striven for so long to keep women away from the sources of power and decision-making which organizational life represents?

One explanation is to consider the power that the 'Goddess' had prior to the rise of the Judaeo-Christian tradition, and to suggest that the last 2000 years have represented men's attempts to keep women in a subordinate position. Maybe men feared the power of women because they could not understand the basis of their intuitive knowing. How else can we explain the degree of male violence directed at women over the centuries? Could this explain the treatment of witches? This may seem a little exaggerated, but it is interesting to note how consistently men have resisted women's attempts to assert themselves and their power, either at home or in the workplace. Riane Eisler writes about this at great depth in her book *The Chalice and the Blade*, and I would recommend this book to anyone wanting to understand female oppression and silence.

Although much has improved over the last twenty years, as ever-increasing numbers of women enter organizations at all levels, many, however, still find themselves ignored, devalued or abused. This is as true in the voluntary and public sectors as in the private sector, but there does appear to have been a more conscious attempt to address the issues of sexism in the voluntary and public sectors. Sexist language and behaviour have been censored, but little has changed in the way of male attitudes.

Only recently a surgeon I was working with insisted on calling his female colleagues, consultant psychiatrists, 'girls', even when I pointed out how offensive this term was when used to refer to mature women. He really could not see why I was making it an issue, and did not believe women would object. He claimed that men at work were known as 'the boys', but I have yet to visit an organization where senior men were referred to in this way. Men on the shop floor might be known as, or even refer to themselves as, 'the lads', but no self-respecting male manager or professional would take kindly to being called a 'boy' by a member of his own or the opposite sex. One is also reminded of the racist connotation of this word when used in the southern states of America, to refer to black men; it certainly denotes a loss of status and power there.

My years of working in training and consultancy have revealed many examples of men abusing their power, or making assumptions about their rights in relation to women at work. As already discussed it is difficult for many women to stand up for their rights at work, whereas men often find this easy, particularly when their job titles give them legitimate power and authority. Men assume women will cater to their needs, be it making the coffee, staying late to finish a report, or listening to their tales of woe.

Many men will invade women's personal space, assuming they have the right to stand as close as they choose, or to touch a woman in an overtly friendly, but often over-familiar, way. This can place a woman in a very difficult position where she may have to tolerate behaviour she does not like because 'the boss' is defining what is acceptable behaviour in the office. She may be labelled a spoilsport, a prude, a feminist, or as having a 'problem'. Men rarely question their own behaviour; they assume that the woman must be the cause of any problem.

Women in paid employment really cannot win; they are seen to be a problem if they conform to the stereotypical views held about them in the wider society, and, equally, a problem if they do not. If a woman takes on board the 'Earth Mother' role, and thus makes herself indispensable to her boss and colleagues, it is more than likely that she will be taken for granted, assumed to have little going for her, and passed over for promotion. Other women may refuse to play this game, but do it in such a way that they become vulnerable to a male backlash. These are the women who are thought to dress inappropriately, by looking too smart or power-ful for their job title, or are seen as prepared to compete with the men on their terms. Such women may be labelled aggressive or unfeminine, and marginalized for not playing the female role according to the male rules.

Many women must feel as though they can't win whatever they do. Having worked in organizations for the past fifteen years I may have a somewhat jaundiced view of men's willingness to change the status quo, particularly as recent cut-backs in these businesses have caused the women, rather than the men, to lose their jobs. It looks increasingly as though one of the best ways forward is for women committed to change to:

* Develop their own support and networks.
* Take time to share their issues and concerns.
* Validate themselves and their perceptions.
* Validate other women's perceptions.
* Understand the difference between 'report-talk' and 'rapport-

talk', and use one which is most appropriate for the outcome desired.

* Develop a range of effective strategies to prevent them from being silenced, in particular assertive techniques.
* Support each other in overcoming difficulties with male employers, colleagues or staff.
* Employ their own consultant to help them deal with these issues.

So what are some of the specific issues for women working with men? The coping strategies I have noted in my male colleagues have included any number of the following:

* Taking control of a situation, by upstaging their female colleague.
* Setting women up to fail, and thus creating situations where they loose credibility.
* Sabotaging a woman who looks as if she might be succeeding.
* Openly putting down women in front of others.
* Excluding women in predominantly male groupings by topic or verbal/non-verbal behaviour.
* Not noticing women's contribution.
* Not listening to women's contribution.
* Demanding attention from women, but rarely giving good attention back.
* Patronizing women in their company.
* Paying attention to and noting a woman's physical attributes rather than responding to the woman's contribution.
* Making jokes at women's expense.

An article in the *Wall Street Journal* called 'Sexual Tension, some men find the office is a little too exciting with women as peers', quoted a young man as saying: 'I find myself spending too much time looking at them and not listening to what they are saying'. This would suggest some support for the above. But what do women have to say about the situation?

A senior member of the management structure of the Midlands Probation Service wrote about her difficulties in trying to challenge and confront male assumptions.

Confronting sexist practice is difficult for women. Individuals who do so can easily become identified as more difficult members of staff. My experience is that my male colleagues become irritated by constant challenge and I fear that when I feel I need to challenge unacceptable behaviour by my male colleagues towards me as a woman I must exercise all my diplomacy skill, otherwise my message either will not be heard or deliberately ignored, as a response to an irritation.[15]

HOW TO PLAY THE GAME

The two main choices for women seem to be either to learn to play like the men, or to stay true to their own values and play the game according to their own rules. The ideal is for women to understand the rules of the game, and so be in a position to choose if and when to (a) play according to them, or (b) play against them.

There are always consequences to our behaviour, and not going by the rules can be quite uncomfortable in the short-term. But as women we are in a position to challenge male rules, and to bring in more humane ways of operating. Many women in management have worked towards an understanding of the rules, keeping within the boundaries at first, and then, having achieved the power and status they require, set about changing the rules. Such women will be helped enormously by the support of other women in the organization.

We will all benefit — women, men and the planet — if we change the rules of the game and introduce more co-operation, concern and honesty. In the meantime we must all develop our assertion and time-management techniques, so that we can handle the inevitable negotiation and conflict situations. The support of a strong network of women is essential too. If a woman respects herself and her values in the workplace, and acts accordingly, there is a good chance she will gain the respect of others and thus help influence daily practice.

8

Working with the Environment

What we do and the way we behave materially affects biological systems on the other side of the planet; we are all connected and we are all interdependent.[1]

So far we have focused on identifying those skills, techniques and strategies necessary for survival in male-defined organizations, but a growing awareness of our need to protect the planet is equally important. We must ensure that our practices at work reflect a sensitivity and concern for environmental issues, and provide a model for others to follow.

THE GREEN PRINCIPLE

The protection of the environment is a precondition of a prosperous, healthy society.[2]

As well as looking after ourselves, it is imperative that we should also act responsibly towards the environment. This may feel like yet another burden for us to carry, but if we, as individual women working within organizations, decline responsibility, who is there to protect Mother Earth? Just as we have a responsibility towards others, we have a responsibility towards the environment; we need to increase our concern for a world that has nurtured us, and our loved ones, for so long. The world is our world too; she is like our sister, and we must treat her with the respect she deserves. According to James Lovelock[3] the earth is alive, a single organism on the surface of which life-forms and the physical environment continually interact to maintain a life-preserving equilibrium – the Gaia hypothesis.

There is no time to lose, given the years of abuse the earth has suffered at the hands of governments, industry and many of the organizations within which we are employed. Men have assumed the right to take what they have wanted from the land, with apparent disregard for the consequences. Can we really afford to remain silent about this injustice any longer? Time is running out; we have to act now.

> Our crises show us the way in which our institutions have betrayed nature. We have equated the good life with material consumption, we have dehumanized work and made it needlessly competitive . . .[4]

Many of us are sensitive to the issues; we know about the exploitation of resources and subsequent pollution from the newspapers and television, yet seem loathe to do anything about it. 'What can *I* do about the destruction of the rainforests, acid rain, global warming, and the pollution of our rivers and seas?' seems to be the common reaction. Our lives are apparently too busy and distressing already to leave us any energy to worry about the effects of environmental damage as well! It's almost as if the enormity of the issue makes us bury our heads in the sand; anything rather than confront this painful reality. And yet if we don't speak out on behalf of Mother Earth, who will? If we don't assume it to be our responsibility, then who will do something to help? We may not intend to pollute the environment but we continue to do so, every day and in numerous ways. If we care enough to want things to change, that change must start with *us*. it is important to realize that 'a fear of knowing is very deeply a fear of doing, because of the responsibility inherent in new knowledge'.[5]

What can we do? In the chapter on Life Planning we put time aside to ask ourselves what we really want from our lives. How about also asking what we can do to help the environment? What do we need to do to ensure the survival of a world which feeds and nurtures us? By taking a step-by-step approach, and gradually making changes, we can protect ourselves from an overwhelming gloom, which can breed depression and inactivity. Apathy damages the soul and widens the divide between action and responsibility. We are just as responsible for our inaction as for our actions, and need to assert ourselves and speak out on behalf of the environment.

According to Confucian writings, wise individuals wanting

good government looked first within, seeking precise words to express their hitherto unvoiced yearnings, 'the tones given off by the heart'. Once they were able to verbalise the intelligence of the heart they disciplined themselves. Order within the self led first to harmony within their own households, then the state and finally the empire.'[6]

The world of work is changing, however, and a recent survey of chief executives of one hundred European companies stated that the greatest pressure to 'go green' came from customers, and pressure from discussions with their children came a close second. Employees (and employers) particularly graduates, are also voting with their feet. Research at one university has shown that 56 per cent of students considered a company's record on environmental issues to be important when selecting potential employers. This will have enormous implications for companies with 'bad' records or in sensitive sectors such as chemicals, waste, oil and so forth. Other surveys suggest that 23 per cent of middle managers would be prepared to move to another company and take a drop in salary for environmental reasons.

So what small steps can we take in the workplace to start making a difference? Certain publications have made an enormous difference to my own behaviour at work and at home; *1001 Ways to Save the Planet* by Bernadette Vallely, *Friends of the Earth Handbook*, *Green Living* by Bernadette Vallely, Felicity Aldridge and Lorna Davies, and *Home Ecology* by Karen Christensen. These are full of practical ideas and hints which help to combat our growing sense of helplessness. Following the practices outlined will enable us all to make a difference. The following pages contain some of their suggestions about ways in which we can start creating environmentally friendly practices, habits and attitudes at work.

An 'A' priority

Learn to view the environment as an 'A' priority, and use a variation of the Swiss cheese method (see page 40). Your sense of satisfaction at seeing the effect of small changes will encourage you to continue working away at the issues.

Given a little bit of energy, knowledge and commitment, individuals can make a big difference.[7]

Attending the conference 'Business, the Leading Edge in the

1990s' at Dartington in 1990 made me stop and take stock of my own practices. Having been sympathetic and active concerning the issues during my years at university, I was shocked and dismayed to realize how little notice I was taking of the impact of my lifestyle on the environment. I was a mass of contradictions, speeding down a motorway, alone in my car, to attend a conference on ecological issues. I had never even stopped to think about taking the train!

Lifestyle audit

As a result, I started to do my own lifestyle audit, and gradually introduced more environmentally sound practices. These included the use of environmentally friendly products, particularly cleaning materials, at home and work, recycling papers and bottles, starting a compost heap in my garden, and buying ecological garden products. Small beginnings perhaps, but they lead to an increased sensitivity and willingness to make other changes. I bought a car with a catalytic converter, started to use the train whenever I could, took out an ethical pension, and was much more thoughtful about my consumption of resources, whether food, household items, clothing or energy. Taking responsibility means starting to do things differently, and realizing your power as a consumer to make producers change their practices.

DEVELOPING AN ENVIRONMENTALLY CONSCIOUS LIFESTYLE

Changes in the office

So what small steps can *you* start to make? Start thinking about the following:

* *Have a smoke-free office*
  This reduces health risks for both smokers and non-smokers, and reduces pollution. It also helps smokers kick the habit.

* *Ventilate your photocopier*
  Ozone can be an indoor pollutant, especially if you work in a room without adequate ventilation near photocopiers that are switched on all day. It can be damaging to mucous membranes and eyes, and can cause headaches.

* *Get a shield or filter for your VDU*
Computer terminals and VDUs emit low-level radiation and have been linked to increasing numbers of miscarriages, headaches and skin rashes. Always take a break after one hour spent in front of the screen.

* *Don't use aerosol cleanser to clean shared office telephones*
The cleaning chemical may be more toxic than your own germs. Just wipe them with a clean, damp cloth.

* *Check office lighting*
White fluorescent strip lights can emit a constant flicker and cause headaches, eyestrain and concentration problems. Where possible use compact fluorescent lighting. These are about the size of ordinary light bulbs but can last for 8,000 hours, and use only one-fifth of the energy for the same output of light. Bernadette Vallely suggests that 'if everyone in Britain replaced just one light bulb it would reduce the need for one power station'.

* *Encourage others to reduce their energy use by:*
 1. Not leaving lights on unnecessarily.
 2. Starting to use compact fluorescent bulbs.
 3. Turning off any machines not in use, especially computers and photocopiers.
 4. Being more efficient in their use of heating.

* *Ask for vending machines to be removed*
Bernadette Vallely suggests that the average vending machine may be the largest single user of energy in the workplace. She advises the use of mugs and low-energy water urns instead.

* *Encourage the use of office equipment with the potential for longer life*
 1. Use secondhand furniture and office equipment when possible.
 2. Use materials like metal filing cabinets, instead of paper or card.
 3. Buy solid wood items from sustainable sources, not rainforest wood.

* *Audit your suppliers*
Ask your suppliers to offer you the best possible alternatives to environmentally damaging products, for instance:

 * recycled paper

* water-based pens
* energy-efficient lighting
* sustainable equipment/furniture

* *Stop using envelopes with plastic windows*
Envelopes with plastic windows are not recyclable and are likely to be made of virgin paper. In contrast, ordinary brown envelopes are mostly made from recycled pulp.

* *Stop using disposable pens*
Disposable pens are made of plastic and are non-biodegradable. Start using a refillable pen, or even pencil.

* *Stop using correcting fluid – unless water-based*
Bernadette says the white correcting fluid contains a chemical 11-trichloroethane, a toxic and irritant chemical that depletes the ozone layer and lingers for a long time in the environment. Look for water-based whiteners that do not contain trichloroethane.

* *Find ways of saving paper*
    * Cut down on the number of photocopies you make
    * Re-use paper written on only one side for notes
    * Always keep a bin next to the copier in which to place spoiled sheets for recycling

* *Find an alternative to clear glues*
Some glues are more toxic than others, and can contain harmful and addictive chemicals. Avoid them wherever possible, and stick to white glues and simple-formula woodworking glues.

* *Don't buy or use coloured paperclips*
These are dipped in bright plastic and contain cadmium, a toxic heavy metal.

* *Use water-based and felt-tipped pens*
Permanent ink markers contain solvents and chemicals which are moderately toxic if swallowed, and should always be used with care in well-ventilated rooms. Prolonged exposure to these chemicals can cause dizziness and affects the central nervous system. Use water-based markers instead.

* *Find alternatives to equipment needing batteries*
The manufacture of batteries uses up to fifty times more energy than the actual energy produced. Move towards mains-operated equipment, and consider using solar-powered calculators,

for example. In the meantime, use 'green' rechargeable batteries, which last up to 500 times longer.

* *Avoid styrofoam coffee cups and plates*
Styrofoam cups, plates and containers should be avoided as they are made with CFCs which destroy the ozone layer, and they cannot be recycled. If there is no other option, use recyclable plates and cups.

* *Install halon-free fire-extinguishers*
Halons are used in certain types of fire extinguishers, particularly those for use on computers and electrical equipment, because they can smother a fire with a foam without destroying the computer. Halon 1211, the chemical usually used, is a serious ozone depleter.

* *Ban aerosols in the office*
By phasing out your use of aerosols, you will not only help the environment, but will probably save money as well. Find alternatives.

* *Demand the provision of disposal facilities for sanitary towels*
Once sanitary towels have been flushed down the toilet, many pass through the sewage system and end up in our seas and on beaches. Insist that alternatives are made available. Remember too, that tampons are environmentally damaging. The cotton is produced only with the help of pesticides and the rayon, derived from wood pulp, is manufactured using chlorine, which forms dioxins as by-products which pollute the rivers and seas. Tampons are not sterilized. Use sanitary pads instead.

* *Develop a system for recycling your waste*
What you may consider rubbish others may well find valuable; discarded computer paper, for example, fetches a good price. Cans, paper, and bottles could be recycled.

* *Support and educate your cleaner*
Give your cleaner training about the harmful effects of various products, and provide him/her with alternative cleansing materials.

* *Create a greener environment in your workplace*
    * have real plants in the office
    * provide recycled products
    * provide alternatives to tea and coffee

* *Support the environment by reassessing your relationship to the car*
They are the most dangerous, uneconomic and environmentally
polluting form of transport ever invented.

> * Say no to a company car unless you absolutely need one.
> * Make sure any car you drive uses lead-free petrol.
> * Insist any new car purchased has a catalytic converter.
> * Install a catalytic converter in your present car.
> * Have your car tested and serviced regularly for fuel econ-
>   omy, safety and minimization of toxic exhaust fumes.
> * Whenever possible travel with a passenger rather than
>   alone.
> * Use the best quality oil for greater efficiency.
> * Go without owning your own car – hire ones if necessary,
>   with catalytic converters.
> * Avoid driving in bad weather; it uses more fuel.
> * Avoid using your car in the city; it wastes fuel.
> * Look after your car – check brakes, oil, and tyres to ensure
>   it is at its most efficient to save fuel and minimize pollu-
>   tion.
> * Plan your trips to save energy.
> * Learn to drive better and in a more energy-conscious way.
> * Avoid extras when buying a car as this increases the
>   amount of engine power needed to run it.
> * Use public transport whenever possible.
> * Walk or cycle short distances.

It is also worth thinking about how we purchase our clothing,
cosmetics and cleansing materials to see if we can be more
environmentally conscious.

Clothes

For instance, we can save energy and money by buying fewer
clothes. Bernadette Vallely claims that in Britain alone we have
over 30 million pounds' worth of clothes left unworn and
unwanted at home. We must be more discerning, and ask ourselves whether we *really* need that new item of clothing.

Dry cleaning is an expensive, polluting and energy-consuming
business. It is always worth checking labels before buying any item
of clothing to ensure that it doesn't need dry cleaning.

Finally, how about recycling your old clothes? Just because you don't like them any more doesn't mean your friends wouldn't appreciate them. You might even be able to sell them at a nearly-new shop, and make some money.

Toiletries

Buy toiletries and beauty products which don't contain dangerous chemicals, and which are cruelty-free. Most make-up is tested on animals unless the label says otherwise. Go for products from The Body Shop or Beauty without Cruelty.

Buy from shops that have environmental policies

As a consumer become more aware — purchase your goods from shops that have stated policies for their own-label produce, and which require high standards from others.

Explore what it means to be a green consumer

Green consumerism means causing less harm to the environment by knowing more and making careful decisions about what you buy. It means making choices which are based on environmental considerations. We need to be wiser in our consumption behaviour and learn to consume less.

> We affect the environment in everything we do, and there are many ways in which we can minimize our effects on our environment without having to alter our life-styles too drastically.[8]

Relevant consumer action

* Supporting organically grown products.
* Encouraging work canteens to provide vegetarian food.
* Supporting the development of an integrated transport system, and the increased resourcing of public transport systems.

In *The Aquarian Conspiracy* Marilyn Ferguson outlined many of the changes she considers necessary to improve economic assumptions and behaviour, and some are listed below. Think how different life and work would be if all these took place:

* Appropriate consumption.
* Conserving, keeping, recycling, quality, intention to serve authentic need.

* Jobs to fit people.
* Co-operation – human values transcend winning.
* Blurring of work and play.
* Co-operation with nature.
* Ecologically sensitive to ultimate cost.
* Logic balanced by hunches, feelings and insights.

As more of us are entering the workplace, we will be in a stronger position to influence the work culture. We shouldn't feel shy about speaking out about unsound practices which harm us or the environment. Most importantly, we need to activate ourselves and take time to educate others, without being tedious or self-righteous.

Energy efficiency in the home

Having made changes at work, how about doing an audit on your home? For example, this could include:

* draught-proofing
* insulating your hot-water tank
* using thermostatic radiator valves to regulate the temperature in each room
* checking all appliances to make sure they are the most energy-efficient, having made sure you really need them in the first place

Measure your house against the model of an ideal *green house*, which would contain the following:

* high level of insulation
* solar water heating
* passive solar heating including a conservatory
* heat recovery from ventilated air and water waste
* collection of rainwater for toilets
* recycling of water for garden use
* building materials chosen for their low environmental impact
* construction materials which are durable, easily repaired and maintained, and easily dismantled at the end of their life

Business practices

Finally, we need to consider the impact of the business we are in on the environment, and see if we are prepared to move on if the organization does not seem willing to consider changing its practices. Some organizations already do take the issue seriously, and we should seek them out. Anita Roddick claims:

> Not a single decision is ever taken in The Body Shop without first considering environmental and social issues. We do not, for example, sell any products which consume a disproportionate amount of energy during their manufacture or disposal, cause unnecessary waste, use ingredients derived from threatened species or threatened environments, or adversely affect other countries, particularly in the Third World. We have an Environmental Projects Department which monitors the company's practices and products to ensure they are environmentally sound and up-to-date . . .[8]

How does your organization compare to this, and what options and choices do you have?

Conclusion

This book provides an opportunity for women considering re-entering the workplace to consider the impact that the changing nature of work will have on their future lives in paid employment.

Women returning to work after a career break, or joining organizational life for the first time, need to appreciate that the move towards leaner organizational structures means that they must think seriously about the skills they have to offer the changing world of work, and those which they may need to acquire. They need to decide which of the various options presented by Charles Handy appeals, and what are the consequences of this choice in the present and the future. For instance, it is likely that everyone wanting careers at the 'core' or operating as 'contract' workers will need to make a life-long commitment to obtaining additional skills and qualifications which can be transferable from one work situation to another. Considerable attention needs to be paid to working out life/career plans and keeping up-to-date with trends in employment. If we act responsibly now, numerous options are open to us; if we choose not to, we must live with the consequences in the future. We need to take responsibility for the lives we want to lead.

This sense of responsibility must also be extended to an awareness of the environment, and in this book Anita Roddick has been identified as one highly visible example of what women can achieve if they have faith in themselves. Anita Roddick values her staff, her customers, her suppliers, the environment and herself. She lives her values, and is a good role model for us all. Many of us still find it difficult to value our 'feminine', given the socialization process we have been subjected to. The important thing to remember, however, is that the very qualities that we take for granted, in ourselves, are those necessary for humanizing the workplace and providing a sense of balance to our ailing organizations and planet. The way forward is a partnership between the male principle (as identified earlier), and the female principle. At present there is too great an emphasis on the male, and insufficient appreciation of the female. We need to assert our feminine, thus improving our self-esteem and enabling the world of work to become more 'person-friendly', and the environment to get the respect it deserves.

The ATS model provides a starting point in that it helps us understand the extent to which everything is interrelated, which is vitally important for the survival of the planet. Whilst many of the ideas and techniques we have explored together have been around for a long time, their value does not diminish. After more than a decade of experience in running training events, I still benefit from reminding myself of the key concepts and techniques in assertion, stress and time management. It doesn't seem to matter how sophisticated we become in coping with organizational life; these are still the key stepping-stones to surviving and potentially thriving in this context.

So what options will we, as working women, have in the 1990s, and beyond. Hopefully, those of us who have felt under attack at work will feel the barriers coming down, and will learn to openly celebrate the feminine. We should honour our interdependence, our co-operation, our emotionality and our intuition. Overall, we should be able to create a better sense of balance in our lives both at work and home, thereby creating a situation in which we have more opportunity for learning to appreciate ourselves, others and the world.

POINTS TO REMEMBER

So what is it we need to hold onto?

Rights
We need to keep reminding ourselves that we have rights in situations; that our needs, opinions and values are important.

The time is now
We need to remember that 'this is not a rehearsal'; this is all there is, and we should get on and make the best use of the life that we have, whilst working towards creating the life that we want.

Taking proper care of ourselves
We must remember to look after ourselves and to build in time for fun, exercise, rest and relaxation.

Respecting ourselves
We need to value our sexuality, and not allow organizations to maintain values and behaviours which dishonour us.

Understanding ourselves
We need to appreciate our major life transitions, in particular the menopause, and help others at home and work give us the help and support we need.

Partnership with men
We need to move towards a more collaborative relationship with men at work, in which the feminine is as valued and nurtured as much as the masculine.

Caring for the environment
We need to change our assumptions about and behaviour towards the environment, and be prepared to challenge others' misuse of it.

It won't all happen overnight, but the change has to start with you! We have to take responsibility for changing ourselves, our lives, the assumptions we have about our rights and the way others treat us at home and work. By standing up for yourself and your values you will be taking control of your life and your future. You benefit, organizations benefit, and the world gets a little healthier too!

Notes

Introduction

1. M. Barrett, *Women's Oppression Today*, 1988.
2. J. West, *Women, Work and the Labour Market*, 1982.
3. Eurostat, a 1981 survey of EEC countries.
4. C. Handy, *Association for Management Education & Development*, June 1991.
5. C. Handy, *op. cit.*
6. C. Handy, *op. cit.*
7. T. Peters, *Thriving on Chaos*, 1989.
8. J. Harvey Jones, *Making it Happen*, 1987.
9. A. Roddick, *Body and Soul*, 1991.
10. J. Marshall, *Patterns of Cultural Awareness as Coping Strategies for Women Managers*, in Sharon E. Kahn & Bonita C. Long (Eds) Coping & Working Women: An Integration, McGill-Queens's Univ. Press, 1991.
11. J. Marshall, *op. cit.*
12. J. Marshall, *op. cit.*

An Introduction to the ATS model

1. Women's Environment Network, 1991.

Chapter 1. ATS – Assertion

1. G. Morgan, *Images of Organization*, 1986.
2. R. Goffe and R. Scase, *Women in Charge: The Experiences of Female Entrepreneurs*, 1981.
3. L. Schierse Leonard, *The Wounded Women*, 1982.

4. A. Townsend, *Assertion Training*, 1985.
5. D. Clarke and J. Underwood, *Assertion Training*, 1988.

Chapter 2. ATS – Time Management

1. S. Wise and L. Stanley, *Georgie Porgie Sexual Harassment in Everyday Life*, 1987.
2. A. Lakein, *How to Get Control of Your Time and Your Life*, 1984.
3. A. Lakein, *op. cit.*
4. F. Kinsman, *Telecommuters*, 1990.
5. A. Lakein, *op. cit.*
6. A. Lakein, *op. cit.*
7. A. Lakein, *op. cit.*

Chapter 3. ATS – Stress Management

1. C. Cooper and M. Davidson, *High Pressure: Working Lives of Women Managers*, 1982.
2. D. Fontana, *Managing Stress*, 1989.
3. D. Fontana, *op. cit.*
4. D. Fontana, *op. cit.*

Chapter 4. Life and Career Planning

1. J. West, *Women, Work and the Labour Market*, 1982.
2. *Women's Organizational Experiences*, LGTB, 1990.
3. R. Goffe and R. Scase, *Women in Charge: The Experiences of Female Entrepreneurs*, 1981.

Chapter 5. Sexuality

1. G. Burrell and J. Hearn, *The Sexuality of Organization*, 1989.
2. A. Phillips, *Menopause: Midlife crisis or cause for celebration*, Guardian 24th September, 1991.
3. R. Moss Kanter, *Men and Women of the Corporation*, 1987.
4. G. Coleman and D. Clarke, *Women's Organizational Experiences*, 1990.
5. D. Sheppard, Organizations, Power and Sexuality: The Image and Self-Image of Women Managers, in *The Sexuality of Organization*, 1989.
6. D. Sheppard, *op. cit.*
7. D. Sheppard, *op. cit.*

8. D. Sheppard, *op. cit.*
9. S. Wise and L. Stanley, *Georgie Porgie Sexual Harassment in Everyday Life*, 1987.
10. S. Wise and L. Stanley, *op. cit.*
11. S. Wise and L. Stanley, *op. cit.*
12. D. Clarke and G. Coleman, *Management Effectiveness for Women*, NEC, 1990.
13. C. Cooper and M. Davidson, *High Pressure: Working Lives of Women Managers*, 1982.
14. A. Sedley and M. Benn, *Sexual Harassment at Work*, 1982.
15. A. Sedley and M. Benn, *op. cit.*

Chapter 6. Managing the Menopause

1. S. Orbach, *Weekend Guardian*, October 1991.
2. A. Phillips, *Guardian*, September 1991.
3. I. Asimov, *Human Body*, 1964.
4. A. Dickson and N. Henriques, *Menopause: The Women's View*, 1987.

Chapter 7. Working with Men

1. J. Marshall, *Patterns of Cultural Awareness as Coping Strategies for Women Managers*, 1991.
2. J. Lever, *Sex differences in the games children play*, 1976.
3. J. Piaget, *The moral judgement of the child*, 1965.
4. J. Lever, *Sex differences in the games children play*, 1976.
5. A. Roddick, *Body and Soul*, 1991.
6. N. Goldberger et al, 'Women's Ways of Knowing – on gaining a voice', *Sex and Gender*, 1987.
7. D. Spender, *Invisible Women*, 1982.
8. K. Horney, 'Towards an understanding of achievement – related conflicts in women', *Journal of Social Issues*, 1972.
9. J. Marshall, *Patterns of Cultural Awareness as Coping Strategies for Women Managers*, 1991.
10. J. Marshall, *op. cit.*
11. N. Goldberger et. al. 'Women's Ways of Knowing – on gaining a voice', *Sex and Gender*, 1987.
12. D. Tannen, *You Just Don't Understand Me*, 1991.
13. A. Miller, *The Drama of Being a Child*, 1987.
14. N. Goldberger, *op. cit.*
15. D. Merchant, *Meeting the Training Needs of Women Senior Officers in the Probation Service*, 1990.

Chapter 8. Working with the Environment

1. *FOE Handbook*, 1990.
2. *FOE Handbook*, 1990.
3. J. Lovelock, *Gaia: A New Look at Life on Earth*, 1982.
4. M. Ferguson, *The Aquarian Conspiracy*, 1982.
5. A. H. Maslow, *Towards a Psychology of Being*, 1968.
6. M. Ferguson, *op. cit.*
7. *FOE Handbook*, 1990.
8. A. Roddick, *Body and Soul*, 1991.

Resources Section

HEALTH

The British Naturopathic and Osteopathic Association
Frazer House, 6 Netherhall Gardens, London NW3 5RR

The British T'ai Chi Chuan Association
7 Upper Wimpole Street, London W1M 7TD

British Wheel of Yoga
1 Hamilton Place, Boston Road, Sleaford, Lincs NG34 7ES

Council for Acupuncture
Suite 1, 19a Cavendish Square, London W1M 9AD

Council for Complementary and Alternative Medicine
Panther House, 38 Mount Pleasant, London WC1X 0AP

The General Council and Registrar of Osteopaths
56 London Street, Reading, Berks RG1 4SQ

Institute for Complementary Medicine
21 Portland Place, London W1N 3AF

The Migraine Trust
45 Great Ormond Street, London WC1N 3HD

National Institute of Medical Herbalists
41 Hatherley Road, Winchester, Hampshire SO22 6RR

The National Osteoporosis Society
Barton Meade House, PO Box 10, Radstock, Bath, Avon BA33 3YB

The Society of Homoeopaths
2 Artizan Road, Northampton, London NN1 4HU

Society of Teachers of Alexander Technique
10 London House, 266 Fulham Road, London SW10 9EL

Transcendental Meditation
Baker Street Centre, 24 Linhope Street, London NW1

HEALTH FARMS

Cedar Falls
Bishops Lydeard, Taunton, Somerset TA4 3HR

Grayshott Hall
Nr Hindhead, Surrey GU26 6JJ

Shrubland Health Clinic
Coddenham, Nr Ipswich, Suffolk IP6 9QH

Springs Hydro
Packington, Nr Ashby-de-la-Zouch, Leicestershire LE6 5TG

SUPPORT

Action on Smoking and Health (ASH)
5–11 Mortimer Street, London W1N 7RH

Association of Carers
21–23 New Road, Chatham, Kent ME4 4QJ

Association for New Approaches to Cancer
5 Larksfield, Englefield Green, Egham, Surrey TW20 0RB

Body Positive Women's Core Group
51b Philbeach Gardens, London SW5 9EB

British Association for Counselling
37A Sheep Street, Rugby CV21 3BX

British Pregnancy Advisory Service (BPAS)
Head Office, Austy Manor, Wooton Wawen, Solihull, West Midlands

Co-counselling International
Westerly, Prestwick Lane, Chiddingfold, Surrey GU8 4XW

Cruse
Cruse House, 126 Sheen Road, Richmond, Surrey

Depressives Associated
PO Box 5, Castle Town, Portland, Dorset DT5 1BQ

The Equal Opportunities Commission
Overseas House, Quay Street, Manchester M3 3HN

Herpes Association
37–41 North Road, London N7

Hysterectomy Support Group
c/o Ann Webb, 11 Henryson Road, Brockley, London SE14 1HL

Lesbian Employment Rights
Room 203, Southbank House, Black Prince Road, London SE1 7SJ

MIND
National Association for Mental Health
22 Harley Street, London W1

The National Association for Widows
Allison Street, Birmingham B5 5TH

Older Feminist Network
c/o AWPA, Women's Place, Hungerford House, Victoria Embankment, London WC2

Positively Women
5 Sebastion Street, London EC1 0HE

Pregnancy Advisory Service (PAS)
11–13 Charlotte Street, London W1

Rape Crisis Centre
PO Box 69, London WC1

Relate
Little Church Street, Rugby CV21 3AP

Re-evaluation Co-counselling
7 Kemble Road, London SE23 1DH

Sisters Against Disablement
2 Mereworth Drive, Duncan Road, London SE8

Terence Higgins Trust
52–54 Gray's Inn Road, London WC1N 8JU

VDU Workers Rights Campaign
City Centre, 35 Featherstone Street, London EC1

Women's Aid
52–54 Featherstone Street, London EC1 8RT

The Women's Alcohol Centre
254 St Paul's Road, London N1

Women's Health and Reproductive Rights Information Centre
52 Featherstone Street, London EC1Y 8RT

Women Returners Network
Chelmsford Adult Education Centre, Patching Hall Lane, Chelmsford, Essex CM1 4DB

Women's Therapy Centre
6 Manor Gardens, London N7

Working Mother's Association
77 Holloway Road, London N7

ECOLOGY

The Body Shop International Plc
Hawthorn Road, Wick, Littlehampton, West Sussex BN17 7LR

Campaign for Lead Free Air (Clear)
3 Endsleigh Street, London WC1H 0DD

Centre for Alternative Technology
Llwyngwern Quarry, Machynlleth, Powys SY20 9AZ

The Ethical Investment Research Services (EIRS)
208–209 Upper Street, London N1 1RL

Friends of the Earth
26–28 Underwood Street, London N1 7JQ

Greenpeace UK
Greenpeace House, Canonbury Villas, London N1 2PN

London Ecology Centre
45 Shelton Street, London WC2H 9HJ

Women's Environmental Network
22 Highbury Grove, London N5 2EA

EDUCATION AND TRAINING

The Dartington Centre
Dartington Hall, Totnes, Devon TQ9 6EL

Findhorn Foundation
The Park, Findhorn, Forres, Grampian IV36 0TS

Hillcroft College
South Bank, Surbiton, Surrey KT6 6DF

The Pepperell Unit
The Industrial Society, Robert Hyde House, 48 Bryanston Square, London W1H 7LN

Redwood Women's Training Association
Invergarry, Kitlings, Walton-on-the-Hill, Staffs ST17 0LE

Women in Management
64 Marryat Road, Wimbledon, London SW15 5BN

Women & Training News
Hewman House, 120 London Road, Gloucester GL1 3TL

USEFUL BOOKS

Alternative Health Care for Women
Patsy Westcott, Thorsons Publishing Group, 1987.

Natural Healing in Gynaecology: A Manual for Women
Rina Nissim, Pandora Press, London 1986

Safer Sex: The Guide for Women Today
Diane Richardson, Pandora, 1990.

Women and the Aids Crisis
Diane Richardson, Unwin Hyman, 1989

In our own hands — a book of self-help therapy
Sheila Ernst and Lucy Goodison, Womens Press, 1984

Inside out, outside in
Louise Eichenbaum and Susie Orbach, Pelican, 1983

Dealing with Depression
K. Nairne and G. Smith, Women's Press, 1984

Coping with Periods
Diana Sanders, W&R Chambers, 1985

Women and Tranquillisers
Celia Haddon, Sheldon Press, 1984

Women Returners' Guide
Linda Stoker, Bloomsbury, 1991.

Networking and Mentoring: A Women's Guide
Dr Lily Segerman-Peck, Piatkus Books, 1991.

Our Bodies, Ourselves — A Health Book by and for Women
Angela Phillips and Jill Rakusen (eds), Penguin 1989

Ourselves Growing Older: Women Ageing with Knowledge and Power
Boston Women's Health Book Collective — Jean Shapiro (British editor)
Fontana Collins, 1989.

Issues of Blood: The Politics of Menstruation
Sophie Laws, Macmillan, 1990.

Protect Yourself: A Woman's Handbook
Jessica Davis, Piatkus Books, 1990.

Aromatherapy: The Encyclopaedia of Plants and Oils and How They Help You
Daniele Ryman, Piatkus Books, 1991.

Herbal Remedies and Home Comforts
Jill Nice, Piatkus Books, 1992.

Daddy's Girls
Zoe Fairbairns, Methuen, 1991.

Bibliography

Bailey, D. and Sproston, C. *Understanding Stress*, HMSO. 1987.

Barrett, M. *Women's Oppression Today*, 1988.

Borysenko, J. *Minding the Body, Mending the Mind*, Bantam, 1988.

Christensen, K. *Home Ecology*, Arlington Books, 1989.

Clarke, D. *Stress Management*, National Extension College, 18 Brooklands Avenue, Cambridge CB2 2HN. Tel: (0223) 316644, 1989.

Clarke, D. and Coleman, G. *Management Effectiveness for Women*, National Extension College, 18 Brooklands Avenue, Cambridge CB2 2HN. Tel: (0223) 316644, 1990.

Clarke, D. and Underwood, J. *Assertion Training*, National Extension College, 18 Brooklands Avenue, Cambridge CB2 2HN. Tel: (0223) 316644, 1988.

Coleman, G. and Clarke, D. *Women's Organisational Experiences*, LGBT, 1990.

Cooper, C. and Davidson, M. *High Pressure: Working Lives of Women Managers*, Fontana, 1982.

Daly, M. *Gyn/Ecology*, The Women's Press, 1979.

Daly, M. *Pure Lust*, The Women's Press, 1984.

Dickson, A. *A Woman in Your Own Right*, Quartet Books, 1982.

Dickson, A. and Henriques, N. *Menopause: The Women's View*, Grapevine, 1987.

Eisler, R. *The Chalice and the Blade*, Unwin, 1990.

Ellis, F. *Green Values: Their Implications for Individuals and Organisations*, Ashridge, 1991.

Eurostat, *Economic and Social Position of Women in the Community*, Luxembourg: EEC, 1981.

Ferguson, M. *The Aquarian Conspiracy*, Paladin Books, 1982.

Fontana, D. *Managing Stress*, BPS Books and Routledge, 1989.

Gendlin, E. *Focusing*, Bantam Books, 1981.

Goffe, R. and Scase, R. *Women in Charge: The Experiences of Female Entrepreneurs*, George Allen and Unwin, 1985.

Goldberger, N., Clinchy, B., Belenky, M. and Taruele, J., 'Women's Ways of Knowing – on gaining a voice', *Sex and Gender*, Sage, 1987.

Greer, G. *The Change: Women, Ageing and The Menopause*, Hamish Hamilton, 1991.

Hadjifotiou, N. *Women and Harassment at Work*, Pluto Press, 1983.

Handy, C. *The Age of Unreason*, Arrow Books, 1990.

Harvey Jones, J. *Making it Happen: Reflections on Leadership*, Collins, 1987,

Hearn, J. et al, *The Sexuality of Organization*, Sage, 1989.

Kinsman, F. *Telecommuters*, W. H. Allen, 1990.

Kinsman, F. *Millennium – Towards Tomorrow's Society*, W. H. Allen, 1990.

Lakein, A. *How to Get Control of your Time and your Life*, Gower, 1989.

Lever, J. *Sex differences in the games children play*, Social Problems, 1976.

Lovelock, J. *Gaia: A New Look at Life on Earth*, Oxford University Press, 1982.

Maslow, A. H. *Towards a Psychology of Being*, Van Nostrand, 1968.

Marshall, J. *Women Managers: Travellers in a Male World*, Wiley, 1984.

Marshall, J. *Patterns of Cultural Awareness as Coping Strategies for Women Managers*, in Kahn and Long (Eds) Coping and Working Women: An integration. McGill-Queen's University Press, 1991.

Merchant, D. *Meeting The Training Needs of Women Senior Probation Officers in The Probation Service*, Masters Degree, Dept Social Policy and Social Work, Univ. Of Birmingham, 1990.

Miller, A. *The Drama of Being a Child*, Virago, 1987.

Morgan, G. *Images of Organization*, Sage, 1986.

Moss Kanter, M. *Men and Women of the Corporation*, Basic Books, 1977.

Pagels, E. *The Gnostic Gospels*, Penguin Books, 1982.

Paul, N. *Developing Personal Effectiveness*, Manpower Services Commission, 1983.

Peters, T. *Thriving on Chaos*, Pan Books, 1989.

Piaget, J. *The Moral Judgement of the Child*, New York, Free Press, 1965.

Plant, J. (ed) *Healing the Wounds: The Promise of Ecofeminism*, New Society Publishers, Philadelphia, 1989.

Porrit, J. (ed) *Friends of the Earth Handbook*, FOE, 1990.

Reitz, R. *Menopause – A Positive Approach*, Unwin, 1981.

Roberts, M. *The Wild Girl*, Methuen, 1984.

Robertson, J. *The Sane Alternative: A choice of futures*, James Robertson Press, 1983.

Roddick, A. *Body and Soul*, Ebury Press, 1991.

Ross, R. *Prospering Woman, A complete guide to achieving the full and abundant life*, Bantam New Age Books, 1982.

Schierse Leonard, L. *The Wounded Woman*, Shambhala, 1985.

Sedley, A. and Benn, M. *Sexual Harassment at Work*, NCCL, 1982.

Shaver, P. and Hendrick, C. (Eds) *Sex and Gender*, Sage, 1987.

Spender, D. *Man made language*, Routledge and Kegan Paul, 1980,

Tannen, D. *You Just Don't Understand Me*, Virago, 1991.

Townsend, A. *Assertion Training*, FPA, 1985.

Vallely, B. *1001 Ways to Save the Planet*, Penguin Books, 1990.

Vallely, B. et al, *Green Living*, Thorsons, 1991.

West, J. *Women, Work and the Labour Market*, Routledge and Kegan Paul, 1982.

Wise, S. and Stanley, L. *Georgie Porgie Sexual Harassment in Everyday Life*, Pandora, 1987.

Index